MW01194778

LIFE SKILLS

FOR

YOUNG MEN

Becoming a son with purpose

By Amy Maryon

Uncopyright

This book is uncopyrighted. No permission is required to reprint, copy, republish, reuse, remix, review, quote or enjoy the text of this book.

Of course, I would appreciate an acknowledgement but it is unnecessary. I operate under God's system for reaping and sowing. I hope my readers would do the same. "Give and it shall be given unto you…"

From the author:

Our society has lost any sort of art for teaching and training our young boys to become men. When did it become unnecessary to perform acts of chivalry? To use basic manners? Or to know how to cook your own food? For some reason, boys are not being taught the necessary skills to become men.

I have created a series for young women to be taught in the areas of keeping house and cooking but I also have four boys to raise and wanted a book for them to learn some basic skills. That is where this book has come from.

I have realized that not every mother out there has a role model for their sons. I hope that this book can give some guidance and insight into areas that you can help your young man explore and grow in.

I pray that it helps you in areas that we as mothers may not be proficient in.

I thank my husband for his guidance in writing this book. He has given me much insight into the "world of men."

Be blessed and enjoy.

Amy Maryon

www.plainandnotsoplain.com

How to use this book

This book has been broken up into weekly sections. There is a total of 18 weeks. It can be counted as ½ a credit hour for home economics if all the skills are utilized and tried.

Week 1
Personal Grooming

As you grow and mature into a man, your sweat glands are also growing, which in turn leads to more body odor as a young adult. To avoid being called "the stinky kid," you can do a few basic things to help prevent this.

Shower

Do this every day. This is your first defense against combating body odor. For best results, wash all of your parts. Start by standing under the water and wetting your hair and the rest of your body. Then grab a quarter sized amount of shampoo and start scrubbing your head. You have to scrub hard on your scalp; otherwise it will collect dandruff type material which can lead to other embarrassing moments with people. Scrub hard, don't be afraid.

Then grab a bath pouf or washcloth and lather up with some body wash or a bar of soap. Start at the top of your body and work your way down. Neck, behind your ears, shoulders, arms, armpits---very important!!!, chest, belly, bottom area and around your privates. Do your legs and feet too—to avoid any foot diseases.

Then stand under the shower head and rinse your entire body from head to toe.

You can shower at night or in the morning, just do it every day. If you tend to do activities at night like wrestle with your brother which cause you to be sweaty, you may want to shower in the morning to avoid smelling .

When you step out of the shower, dry your body thoroughly before putting on any clothing.

Getting dressed

Just as it is important to shower each day, you need to put on clean clothing every day as well to avoid body odor. If you don't know if something is clean do the "sniff-test" especially in the armpit area. You will be able to tell real quick whether it is dirty or not☺

Take note if during the day you do a lot of sweating and are in need of changing your clothing. Maybe you have been working in work boots all day and your feet are sweaty, it is important to change your socks to keep your feet dry as much as you can. If you have been sweating, putting a fresh t-shirt on will help you combat any unwanted odors as well.

I know at your age, you probably are not thinking much about your appearance, many guys don't. But it is important to be considerate of the people around you and who have to travel in the car with you. No one wants to sit near the "stinky kid."

Shaving

Shaving can be a challenge when you're first starting out, but with a few simple tips you can be on your way to doing the perfect shave.

1. Before you shave, wet your skin and beard to soften it. Taking a shower is a great way to soften your skins' hair.
2. Next, apply a shaving cream or gel. Squirt about a golf ball size foam onto your hands and spread on your beard or mustache area. Shave gel helps prevent razor burn, if you have a choice,get this.
3. Take your razor and shave in the direction that the hair grows. You may have to go over the area a few times to remove stubborn hair. Don't press hard, a good razor will do all the work.
4. If you have to dip your razor in water to remove foam in between swipes, then do so. Shake it off before shaving your face again.
5. Rinse with cold water when finished to remove excess shave cream.

Change your blades or throw away disposable razors after 5-7 shaves to help minimize irritation. You will notice that the blades do not shave as well or they begin to start tugging when you're shaving... this means they are going bad.

Use a multi-blade razor and you will get a smoother shave. The first blade cuts the hair, but it also lifts it out of the skin; the next blades cut progressively closer, enabling fewer strokes and leaving a closer shave with less irritation.

Note that if you have acne, take special care while shaving. Shaving can irritate your skin and make acne worse. Never try to cut over top of pimples, it will make them worse.

If you have access to an electric razor, it is much milder on your face. You can pretty much move it around and not worry about cutting your face☺

Razor burn

What is it?

Razor burn is a skin irritation that is caused by many different factors while shaving. It usually happens after a few moments of shaving and can be in the form of rash. Here are some factors that can cause razor burn:

Dry shaving

Always use a shave cream. They are made to hydrate your face and the hairs on your face. This will help your razor glide across and can hold in hydration while you shave.

Pressing too hard

Being overly aggressive with your razor is a quick way to get razor burn. Let the razor do the work for you.

Change your blades

If your blades are dull, swap them out. This will help in non irritation while shaving.

What are some ways to help get rid of the razor burn while your face is healing up?

- apply some aloe vera gel either from an aloe vera leaf or a bottle
- apply an astringent liquid such as witch hazel, apple cider vinegar, or a combination of 2-3 drops of tea tree oil and 1 Tablespoon of water

How about shaving nicks?

No matter how careful you may be, you are bound to get a small nick sooner or later while shaving. Most men just use small pieces of toilet paper applied to the little wounds and they wait for them to clot up. This is an effective way to stop it, but sometimes it takes a much longer time. What else can you do? Here are some different options for when you experience this:

- aftershaves—the alcohol in aftershaves acts as an astringent and can help slow bleeding
- applying witch hazel-works as an antiseptic which can prevent skin infections
- applying cold water—it will cause your blood vessels to constrict, which will cause the blood vessels to slow and eventually clot.
- lip balm- like chap stick—the waxy texture will help seal the wounds allowing a clot to form
- anti-perspirant—dab anti-perspirant on wound. The aluminum chloride will act as an astringent.
- Vaseline or petroleum jelly—apply a small amount as you do the chap stick---(remove before you leave the house☺)

- Mouth wash---yes the stuff used to make your mouth all fresh and clean started out as a surgical antiseptic and was used to clean wounds on battlefields of WWI
- just apply pressure---if all else fails, apply pressure to the area and it should stop within a few minutes.

Lotion

Lotion is NOT just for girls. You can use lotion to keep from having dry, flaky, and itchy skin. You can get lotion made especially for guys. It doesn't have to have all the "girl" smells added to them. If you put it on while you are still damp after a shower, it will be a smoother process.

Deodorant

Another possible thing to use to help fight the body odor is to apply deodorant daily. If you want a natural choice, choose ones that say deodorant. The ones that say anti-perspirant/ deodorant contain some chemicals that block your sweat glands. Some would argue that this was not good for you. I have had men in my life use both kinds, some were able to use just the deodorant kind and not smell and the others have used that kind and it did not work at all. You have to use your own judgment. Try different brands to find a smell that works for you.

Cologne

Why wear cologne?

There are two main reasons: backup for deodorant and personal scent. When you get hot in certain places on your body, the odor protection that deodorant provides starts to break down. That's why you have cologne in reserve to mask the natural body scents that people are going to find offensive.

How much to apply?

Regulate the number of spritzes. One to two is enough when applying to the body.

Where to apply?

You want to apply where your body generates the most heat. When you do this, the cologne will "activate" when you need it throughout the day. Some examples include:

- wrists
- underarms
- neck
- chest
- thighs
- back

Hand washing

This is important to discuss because it is about personal hygiene as well as preventing sickness and disease. When you touch things and they are contaminated with germs, everything else you touch becomes contaminated. It is important to do this, especially after using the bathroom, before eating, before working with food, or handling any type of animal.

How to wash your hands:

Seems silly to address this, there is a reason that there are signs in restaurant bathrooms on how long to wash your hands for☺ It takes 15-20 seconds to wash your hands under warm water with soap. Take note of your nails to see if you need to use a brush to remove dirt under them, which can also contain germs. Make sure to dry thoroughly afterwards with a towel or air dryer.

Hair care

We have already discussed the importance of washing your hair daily. Young men usually have oil problems, and to wash each day is a good idea.

Some boys use gels or mousse to help style their hair. These generally wash out easily.   If you have very long hair and find it hard to untangle...use a conditioner to help the comb go through your hair much easier.

Get a haircut that is easy to style. Less fuss is always easier.

Ears

Most people will recommend not to insert a cotton swab to clean your ears. If you don't do that in your home, use a washcloth with your finger inserted in your ear to clean out any wax. When you scrub your body, remember to scrub behind your ears, where dead skin will accumulate.

Teeth

The best way to take care of your teeth is to brush them. Here are some tips:

- Pick the right brush. A brush with bristles labeled "medium or hard" will be too tough and can actually contribute to gum disease. A worn out toothbrush won't get your teeth squeaky clean. Replace every three months.
- Use toothpaste that contains fluoride, which helps prevent cavities.
- When you are finished brushing all surfaces of your teeth, brush your tongue. This can hold bacteria that can make your breath smelly.
- You need to brush for 2-3 minutes to get them done well.
- Always floss. Most cavities are found in between the teeth, which can't be reached with a brush.

Bad breath

If you keep your teeth properly brushed, brush your tongue, and floss your teeth regularly you should have fairly decent breath. You can always suck on a few mints to help freshen up your breath.

Drink plenty of water to flush bacteria out of your mouth. You can always breathe into your cupped hand and smell it to see if your breath stinks. Keep a pack of mints on hand for public outings☺

Feet care

Feet can be one of the smelliest parts of your body along with those armpits☺ This is because these two areas sweat a lot. When bacteria are allowed to grow, they emit an unpleasant odor. Foot care is just like caring for any other part of your body. Keep it clean and dry.

A common foot problem is athlete's foot. This can turn your feet into an itchy, smelly mess. It looks like you have extra dry skin on the bottom of one or more of your toes. It can usually be treated with an antifungal spray. It is important to get rid of this right away because this can spread to other parts of your body. Have you ever heard of jock itch ? It can affect that area.

Nail care

If you have ever shaken hands with someone with bad fingernails, it is definitely something you will remember about that person. Men sometimes tend to bite their fingernails which will cause an uneven jagged look. Take an extra minute or two and use a fingernail clipper to clean up your fingernails and toenails.

Cut across the top of the nail and then do the sides slightly. You will have to do some minor clips to get the sides as even and rounded as possible. You don't want pointed corners.

Acne

I know this part of your life is hard, most EVERY teenage boy gets acne, and it's just the natural part of growing up. All those hormones are changing and it causes bodily changes within. You experience stress and unhealthy eating habits and bam!!! you have a breakout. So what can you do to help prevent some of them??

Eat a healthy diet. I know I am talking to a wall right now, but what types of food you put into your body, you are going to get out of it. Try to limit the amount of greasy salty foods, fast foods, and sugar filled drinks. Increase the amount of fresh fruits and vegetables that you eat.

Drink lots of water. The only way to flush out those toxins is to wash them away. Just pure, plain water. Don't buy those sugar filled drinks. Keep a water bottle with you and keep filling it. Drink 4-5 of these a day at least.

Exercise. Causing your body to sweat and allowing it to release those toxins within your body is a good thing. The next step is to SHOWER as quickly as possible after a workout to remove those oily germs off your body. Put on clean clothing afterwards.

Wash your face, neck, and back every day. After showering apply a product like an Astringent. Apply it with a cotton ball and wipe your acne prone areas. You will see the dirt and oil left on your body even after you shower. This costs only about $2 at your local store.

Avoid touching your face with your hands throughout the day, if possible to avoid spreading any germs.

If you are experiencing extreme acne you can talk to your doctor about other products that may help. Remember it starts from within. Instead of going and getting a heavy duty chemical to put on your face, start taking care of yourself properly and heal your acne on your own.

What about back acne

Some men because of the sebaceous glands on their backs coupled with hair and several other factors, are susceptible to this difficult form of acne.

This can be embarrassing for a young man especially when going swimming. It is easily treated; it just needs some constant attention. Here are some tips:

- Check to see if your soaps are causing the pores to be clogged. Sometimes scented ones clog pores. Try a natural body wash specifically for acne.
- Shower daily and keep dry. If you work out, change your shirt.
- Change your sheets weekly along with your pillowcase to help prevent acne.
- Wear a clean cotton shirt while working out and shower afterwards. Don't sit around for hours with your sweaty shirt to breed bacteria and cause breakouts.

Week 2
Manners and social skills

How to shake hands properly

This is going to be an important thing that you learn to do. First impressions are very big in our world and you ALWAYS want to make a good one. You never know who will be watching you to get a recommendation for a job, maybe a new friendship, or perhaps a girl interest.

Steps for doing a proper handshake:

1. Stand and look the other person in the eye before shaking hands. If you are being introduced to someone, stand up and look them in the eye and shake hands. This shows respect and puts you at the same level as the other person. Making eye contact and offering a sincere smile shows you are happy to be where you are. Be still and face the other person to prevent giving the impression that you are in a hurry to get away.
2. Offer a greeting while shaking hands with the other person. "It is so nice to meet you, Mr. Smith." You should include the person's name and offer your name if they don't know it.
3. If your hands are sweaty, wipe them on your pants before offering your hand.
4. Your handshake should be firm not crushing to the person. Be firm but not overpowering--- that shows confidence.

5. Shake in an up and down motion. It should last from 2-5 seconds. If it is awkwardly longer, you can gently pull away politely while maintaining a pleasant expression.
6. To help you remember the person's name easier, say it in the greeting and another time in the conversation to help remember it. In your mind place it with an image to help you remember it easier.

Eye contact and what it says about you

An important thing to remember in social situations is to have good eye contact. If you aren't looking at the person who is talking to you or who you are talking with, it shows that you are not interested. People like to think that you are generally interested in what they have to say. It is important to give eye contact when speaking to someone.

This is also true in a business situation or a social gathering. It makes you look confident and sure of yourself. Show that you care about the person to whom you are talking with by showing eye contact.

How to introduce yourself in various situations

1. Make eye contact. This shows that you are open to attention from someone else. If you are in a group setting, make periodic eye contact with those who are in the group.
2. Smile. It is important to be genuine and happy when you meet someone. This will help share in the positive experience.
3. Use appropriate good body language. Mirror the body language of people around you. Stand with your head high and your back straight. Don't slouch.

4. Say in a pleasant tone, "Hello or Hi, my name is Evan. What's your name?" Then repeat their name by saying, "It's nice to meet you, Sarah."
5. Offer a handshake if appropriate.
6. Ask questions. You may tell a little bit of your background and what you enjoy doing. This is appropriate and may lead to further discussion. Don't take this opportunity to only talk about yourself. You will come across as selfish and uninteresting.
7. Close the conversation. Say something like, "Sarah, it was very nice to meet you and I hope to see you around."

How to introduce other people

1. First, state the name of the person being introduced to. This would be the "higher ranking" person.
2. Say, "I would like to introduce to you, Michael"
3. State the name of the person being introduced "Michael, let me introduce you to Paul.
4. Finally, offer some details about each person, as appropriate.

Typically this is the rank in how to introduce:

- An older person to a younger person
- A business professional to a worker
- A customer to a sales team
- A guest to a host

How to properly order food and what to avoid

If you are indecisive about eating at a restaurant, most offer online menus. Browse the menu beforehand to help choose what you will eat for your meal. If you aren't ready to order when your server is standing there, simply tell them you need more time. Holding them there as you change your mind is not good manners.

The signal that shows you are ready is a closed menu.

It is fine to tell the server that you would like to share an appetizer, dessert, or possibly a main course if you know the servings to be huge. Just remember to give an extra tip, as the order would have been more if two plates were ordered.

Some foods to avoid: Lobster, crab in the shell, unboned fish, and pastas that may be messy or difficult to eat---they could make more demands on your time and concentration than you would like. Think twice about ordering an unfamiliar plate.

How to leave a tip

The standard amount of a food bill is 15% of your total. You can always leave more if the service was above and beyond that. Never leave less, it is tacky.   Waitresses do not get paid normal per hour pay, they earn off tips.

Tip more:

- if you have a large group of people
- your order required several trips to the kitchen or was complicated

- you stayed for a considerable amount of time
- your waitress service exceeded your expectations

How to think of something to say in a conversation

When talking to someone one-on-one, this may lead to an array of awkward silences. Here are some tips to help avoid this:

- Don't think any question is too generic. If the conversation is awkward, get the ball rolling with any question. "Seen any good movies lately?" "What do you do for fun?"
- Elaborate on the things you have to say. If it is your turn to talk, instead of saying "fine" or "It was good." Give more opinions to your answer. Stretch out your time to speak to keep the conversation rolling.
- Pay attention and keep up with the conversation going on around you. It is much easier to come up with things to talk about when you really follow along with what everyone else is saying. Usually something relevant you can add will pop into your mind, sparked by a statement made by someone.

Let's say you are in a conversation that you know nothing about. There are some things you can do. Instead of saying "Uhhhhhh……" and scrambling for something to say, just say "Ha, ha, sorry. I don't know much about that stuff."

Conversation approaches

- Be curious about other people and make it your goal to find out what's interesting and unique about them. This is important for you to be a good listener in the conversation. Let them talk as you discover new things about them.

- Talk in terms of their interests. Keep the conversation rolling by asking questions based on the things they are discussing.
- Try and hit a topic that you both naturally want to talk about. This will help you be more involved with your conversation.

How to make friends

This is hard for some, especially those who have moved to a new place. To make friends, here are some tips.

- Being friendly. Waving, smiling, or cracking jokes with them. These are all beginning ways to have contact with others. Be interested in your potential new friend. Ask him questions about his likes and dislikes, how things are going for them, or what kinds of things he likes to do.
- One way of growing a friendship is to do things together. Activities that don't really interact can't help you to get to know them well. Try going to the park, on an outing, or building something together.
- If you want to change crowds, try getting involved in some other activities. Attending some library programs or a youth activity at church are other ways of meeting friends.

Meal manners

It takes much time and effort to have an attractive table and a tasty meal. When a cook prepares a meal, you should respect the time and effort by coming to the meal with a decent appearance, a grateful attitude, and careful consideration for the others dining. Slouching in your chair, displaying a grumpy, negative spirit, and being thoughtless or selfish can ruin an otherwise wonderful meal.

No one enjoys eating with someone who wolfs his food down, slurps his soup, talks with his mouth full, and burps loudly. Manners are common courtesy shown to others so that everyone can enjoy delicious food in a pleasant atmosphere. If you practice using good manners at every meal, you won't be embarrassed on special occasions by not knowing what to do.   You also won't be caught off guard when someone suggests that you are being rude from a daily habit that you should not be doing.

Our family mealtime should be one of the most pleasant times of our day. We should engage in good conversation instead of monotone answers.

Here are some things to remember when eating a meal with family

- Sit up and remember to bring the food to your mouth.
- Wait for a lull in the conversation to ask politely for food.
- Answer questions pleasantly.
- Be alert to requests from other family members.
- Use your napkin.
- If you are missing something, like a fork, get up and get it yourself.

Using appropriate humor is also good at the table, it creates a happy mood. Avoid teasing and jokes at this time. Don't use it to beg for requests of your parents. It is a good time to discuss current events, things that are important at your church, and maybe some interesting things that happened during the day.

Whoever is responsible for making the meal, be sure to THANK THEM. Even if you did not enjoy something, thank them for taking the time to make the food for you to eat. Always help CLEAN UP AFTERWARDS. Ask what it is you can do before they have to tell you what you can do.

Rules for when you are a guest in someone else's home (many will apply to home life as well):

- Leave your personal problems at home. Don't use this time to discuss negative things going on in your life.
- Stand behind your chair and wait to sit down until the hostess sits down.
- If you are a boy, you should help the girl sit in her chair.
- Keep your hand in your lap when not using it instead of on the table.
- When food is passed take a moderate helping, keeping in mind there are others eating.
- Lay your utensils on your plate when taking a drink.
- Cut your food into small pieces. Place your knife across the top of your plate in between cutting.
- Use your napkin frequently, which should be in your lap.
- Chew slowly and quietly with your mouth closed. Swallow your food before you begin to talk.
- Wait to begin eating until the hostess begins passing the food. Pass it to your left. Pass all the food before you begin eating.
- Bread or rolls should be torn apart and butter should be placed on it as you eat it.
- When eating soup, spoon should be brought up away from you, then into your mouth.

- When you are finished eating you should place your knife and fork across the middle of your plate. Place your napkin to the left of your plate.
- If an accidental spill occurs, instantly offer to help clean it up.
- Engage in lively conversations with your hostess, try and get others to talk about things, not much about yourself. Avoid topics of confrontation. Make things pleasant.
- Do not leave the table before your hostess does. Always ask to be excused before leaving the table.
- Sit up straight, both feet on the ground or have your legs crossed.
- If all else fails and you are not sure what to do during a meal, follow your hostesses lead.
- You can follow up with a thank you card or a quick phone call of thanks.

Some miscellaneous social skills and manners

It is GOOD manners to open a door for another person. If you open it for a girl, make sure to hold the door open for anyone else that may go through. Pay attention to elderly, moms with strollers, or anyone else needing assistance.

You can open the door for a girl when they enter your vehicle. Make sure to check that they are completely in the car before you shut the door.

It is proper to wait to sit down until all the girls or hostess is sitting down at the table when eating.

It is NOT proper to spit, hack, or snort mucous around other people, especially young ladies. It may be a "guy" thing, but keep it that way. Nothing is worse than seeing a young man "spit" out his window when walking by. Yuck!!!

Burping, farting, and any other body noise is also prohibited if you want any kind of positive attention on yourself.

Your conversation should be proper when speaking with others as well. If you are careless with your words it will say a lot about who you are. The Bible states…" out of the abundance of the heart the mouth speaks." Be careful what you are filling your heart with.

Pay attention to elderly people when you are at shopping centers. See if they need assistance taking their shopping carts or riders back up to the store. Being aware of someone besides you is a good thing.

I won't go into the obvious things to avoid—smoking, vaping, drugs, and drinking. These are all "traps" that will only lead to a lifelong bondage. Even if it looks cool, I guarantee that to "potential prospects" it DOES NOT look good. Ask anyone who is addicted to a drug and they will say how hard it is to quit when they are older. It is a bondage that you do not want to get started with.

Some things to look up on your own:

- Know at least one good, clean, and funny joke to share.
- Know how to give a compliment: Be sincere, be specific.
- Make a brief speech in public without having an anxiety attack.
- Pray aloud in a large group—practice praying for your family at meal times.
- Recite the 10 commandments from memory. If you remember these and follow them, you will save yourself much self -inflicted damage that could potentially mess up your future.
- Recognize when you are boring someone with your conversation.
- Endure an insult with grace.

- Learn to not be offended or to take offense. If you are secure in your position in life and know where God has you, then you have no reason to take offense at someone inquiring about what you do.
- Admit being wrong in a situation.
- Learn to say "I'm sorry, and Please forgive me." This will save you much heartache in marriage.
- Take harsh criticism without being defensive—this goes along with offenses.
- Recognize wisdom and how to get it.

Recognize the difference between love and lust—avoid the latter.

Week 3
Cleaning your room

This week we are focusing on being devoted. A good place to begin being devoted is by maintaining a clean bedroom. I know the whole persona of "I am a teen and a guy, I am going to have a messy room like the rest of the world," may seem cool, but in reality it only creates chaos in your life. How many times do you go looking for that outfit or that thing and can't seem to find it? It is best to learn how to keep a room that is clean and orderly.

This week you will be learning how to declutter, organize, and clean your room.

Declutter

You will need the following for this task:

- a box for donating
- a trash bag for garbage
- a basket for items that go elsewhere in the home
- a wet rag for wiping out the insides of things

Almost everyone owns too many things, unless you are a minimalist. But even a minimalist can acquire too much and will need to weed out every once in a while. Before you begin you will need a clean workspace to work at in your bedroom. I recommend using your bed as your work zone.

Start with an article of furniture like a night stand. Begin by emptying out all of the drawers and shelves and putting the items onto your bed.   Start looking through and grabbing the trash items and throwing them away. Don't keep things that are broken, or of no value. If you find things that go in other areas of the home like paper clips, books, or items you borrowed, put them in the basket to go elsewhere. Look at your items and decide if you no longer have use for them. A good way to tell is if you haven't done anything with it for over a year. After you have sorted through your pile, wipe out the inside of your drawer to remove any dust or dirt. You can then begin by organizing and placing your items back inside.

You are going to move in a clockwise pattern as you work your way around your room decluttering and organizing. If your bed is next, start by removing everything that is underneath it. Do the same process that you did for cleaning out the nightstand.

Let's start on your dresser. Remove all items off the top of your dresser. Place anything that does not belong here and place it in its proper place. If you have a jar for coins, put all the coins inside of that. Throw away pieces of trash. There shouldn't be a whole lot of things on top of your dresser, keep it clean and neat.

If you don't have to have an item out, put it away. You want to have things looking neat and clean. When the top of your dresser is clean, begin by going through your drawers.

Take each drawer and dump it on your bed. Go through all of your clothing, throw out any ripped, stained or any items that are too small. If you have some that need repairs, set them in a separate pile. Make a note to repair them. If you haven't worn the item in a year, donate it. Keep only what you like to wear and feel comfortable in. Wipe out the insides of your drawers before putting items back into them. Fold each item and place them back in the drawers neatly.

For bookshelves take all of the items off. Go through the books and decide which ones you want to keep and which ones to donate. Wipe off the shelves and place all the books back on the shelves. Put them back in some sort of order. Sort them according to the types of books. If you have school books, put those together. Fiction books, put them together. Place them all vertical on the shelf. This creates a taller, more organized looking shelf. Any CD's or DVD's go through and decide if you want to keep them out. If you have them on your music player and don't need them out, put them away in a box under your bed or in the closet.

You have probably moved around most of your room, keep going until it is done and then we move on to the biggest, probably the messiest----your closet!

Take everything out of your closet. Use your rag and wipe out the inside corners and any shelves to remove cobwebs and dust. If you have carpet, vacuum the corners and cracks.

Now go through the clothing. Throw out old, ripped, and stained clothing. Anything that is too small, put it in the donate box. If you have any that needs repairing, put it in the pile to be mended. Then, start sorting the different types of clothing that you have in piles. Put all your t-shirts, your long sleeve shirts, and any button up shirts , into separate piles. This will help you to have some order in your closet. It will also help you to see if you have one too many of something ☺ . Put them back in your closet. Put the items that you don't frequently use towards the back. This can be jackets, suits used for special occasions, or out of season clothing. Then put your clothing in a pattern. Do tank style shirts, t shirts, long sleeve shirts, and dress shirts, in that order. You can also take it one step further and within the t-shirts, sort them according to color. This helps give you an organized look to your wardrobe. It will also help you determine which types of items that you need when you do have to go shopping for clothing.

If you keep your shoes in your closet, depending upon how many of shoes you own, you can either neatly set them out on the bottom or purchase a shoe rack. These are fairly inexpensive at the store and it holds many pairs of shoes.

Use the top of your closet to hold seasonal items such as gloves, hats, scarves, etc. You can get inexpensive boxes or baskets to hold these items.

Depending upon how cluttered your room is, this may take you a few hours or a few days. Just keep at it. Go through all of your room, and don't stop until you are finished. Being organized is a positive trait to be able to function without chaos in life.

Cleaning

You have decluttered, and organized, now it is time to clean. Get out some basic cleaning supplies:

- Vacuum
- Wood cleaner---with a rag and bucket (if necessary)
- Window cleaner and rag
- Broom---for cleaning spider webs off ceiling
- Bucket with all purpose cleaner and water for wiping walls, heating vents, etc and a rag
1. **Removing cobwebs**. Start by taking your broom and going around all of the corners of your ceiling and removing any cobwebs that may be hanging.

2. **Wiping walls**. Grab your bucket with all purpose cleaner and begin wiping the walls of your bedroom. Start at the top and move down. That way, if any drips occur, you can wipe it as you are moving down.

3. **Overhead fans**. Carefully wipe each individual blade with water and cleaner. These are probably really dirty.

4. **Window treatments**. If you have curtains, take them down and wash them. Hang them up wet and tug down on them as they are drying. If you have blinds, you can take them down and wash them in a bathroom---it takes some time, but you only have to do this once per year. Or you might choose to hose them off outside. Wipe each one individually.

5. **Windows.** Use your cleaner and clean the windows. When you are finished, take and wipe anything else like mirrors, computer screens, TV screens, and phone screens.

6. **Miscellaneous things.** Don't forget to wipe window sills, heating vents, light switches, door knobs, and closet handles.

7. **Flat surfaces**. Anything that you didn't wipe off already, wipe. Pay attention to all of the edges and sides.

8. **Floors**. Give your room a thorough vacuuming. Move in a pattern. Start on one side and vacuum every area. If you need to move furniture, do that. Get underneath the dressers and nightstands. Take the hose and vacuum underneath bed. Concentrate on all of the cracks and corners. Continue moving until you have finished the entire surface of the floor.

9. **Wash bedding**. Remove all of your bedding and wash it. If you are able to hang it outside, let it air dry. There is something about climbing into bed and enjoying the smell of line, dried sheets.

10. **Air out your room**. If it is cold, open your windows and shut your bedroom door. Let your room air out for 15 minutes or longer.
11. **Make your bed.** Tuck in the sheets and blankets at the foot of your bed. Have your comforter lay evenly on all sides of your bed.

To finish up your room, take your trash bag and throw it away. Immediately go and return all of the items that are to be placed elsewhere in your home. Don't just set it down somewhere, put it all away. Put away all of your cleaning tools where they belong. Rinse out the bucket if needed. Take your donate box and set it by the door to take with you as you leave the home next time.

How to vacuum

Vacuuming is about thoroughly doing the entire floor of carpet. It is easy to skip around the edges or underneath objects, because you do not see them. What can happen is that you may notice a darker line around the edge of your room. That is dirt that has accumulated and usually it is where the edge of your vacuum reaches. The best way to get rid of that is by getting your crevice/edge tool and attach it to your vacuum. Go around the entire corners of your room. Move in a clockwise pattern. Remember to go underneath furniture that cannot be moved. After you have done the edges, start on the surface of the floor. Move in a left to right, back to front pattern. You need to go over the carpet more than one time to make sure that all of the dirt has been picked up. Do it slowly, to give the machine time to suck up the dirt. If you notice that it is leaving some pieces behind, check to make sure that your vacuum doesn't need cleaning out. It is pointless to continue vacuuming if it isn't picking up all of the dirt. Stop, and take the time to clean it out. Finally work your way out of your door.

Then you can stand back and enjoy a freshly vacuumed carpet. It may only last for a few seconds, but for a moment you can enjoy.

First aid basics

Part of growing up is knowing what to do in an emergency. Being mature and able to be depended on when an emergency arises is a blessing for everyone.

Here are some basic first aid skills that you should know:

Puncture wound or cuts and scrapes

If a person has a small puncture, cut, or scrape it may or may not bleed. Here are some steps to take care of it:

1. Wash your hands, to prevent spreading infection.
2. Apply pressure to the wound to stop the bleeding.
3. Clean the wound with clear water. Remove any debris with tweezers. Make sure to clean the tweezers in alcohol first. If debris still remains, see a doctor. Carefully clean the area around with a washcloth and warm water.
4. Apply an antibiotic. Applying a thin layer of cream can help stop spread of infection.
5. Cover the wound with a bandage.
6. Change the dressing as it becomes wet or dirty.

7. Watch for signs of infection. If it doesn't heal, has more pain, is red or has any discharge, see a doctor.
8. If the bleeding does not stop or appears to be very deep, it may need stitches. See a doctor.

Burns

These can be serious or in most cases not so bad. If you have a small burn just on the surface of the skin from touching a hot object, immediately place the area under cool running water. Keep the area covered in water until it feel better about 10-15 minutes.

If the area blisters, don't break them. Cover them with antibiotic cream and a bandage.

If you develop large blisters, see your doctor. If you notice signs of infection such as oozing from the wound or increased pain, redness or swelling see your doctor.

For severe burns, call 911 immediately.

Bug bites or stings

Most reactions to bites are mild, causing only discomfort to a person. But in some cases it can cause an allergic reaction. For most, wash the area with soap and water. If there is a stinger, remove that. Apply a cold pack to reduce pain and swelling. Use a pain reliever if necessary. Apply a topical cream such as hydrocortisone to ease the pain and relieve any itching. Take an antihistamine, such as Benadryl, if you are experiencing an allergic reaction to the bite.

For a severe reaction such as difficulty breathing, swelling of the lips or throat, faintness, dizziness, confusion, rapid heartbeat, nausea, cramps, or vomiting contact a doctor or 911 immediately.

Heat exhaustion

This is sometimes common with little children who have been outdoors playing in the hot sun for an extended period of time. They may begin to start feeling faint or dizzy. They might have a headache, feel fatigued, or have many other abnormal symptoms. The best thing to do is if you notice they are acting differently is to get them indoors out of the sun. Try and get them in an air conditioned room. Remove any tight clothing and elevate the legs and feet slightly. Give them cool drinks to sip on while you sponge their bodies gently with a cool wet cloth. If they don't seem to be getting better, call 911 or your doctor immediately. This can lead to heat stroke.

Frostbite

At the other extreme, if you are outdoors in the winter time you can be exposed to frostbite in extreme temperatures. It is very important to have all of your skin unexposed while venturing out in to the blistery weather. Even if the weather is fair and you are having little ones outdoors to play, it is important that if their hands get wet with snow, you bring them indoors and change their gloves immediately. I like to keep my gloves off and in my pockets and I know that if I am freezing than my little ones are probably cold as well. They won't as likely tell you that they are cold, so it will be your job to only let them play for increments of time outdoors in the winter. When you bring them back indoors, do not put their hands in warm water. It will only cause them to burn. Gently massage them together to warm them up.

Falls or head trauma

These are all sensitive issues and as with everything use caution. If my child is to fall down, I usually let them try and get themselves up. If they are able to stand up, even partially, then I know that the fall is not that severe. Do not pick up a child who has fallen and lays there. You don't want to do more damage to them in case something is broken. Carefully try and calm the child down and see if you can find out where the pain is coming from. If crying continues for an extended period of time, ½ hour to 1 hour, I would suggest calling 911 or visiting your nearest ER. If the child can be comforted within a matter of moments, they will probably be alright. Don't immediately give a child pain relieving medicine, especially after a head trauma. Give their bodies some time to figure out what is going on and if you don't need to visit the ER, you can administer a dose to make them more comfortable.

Bumps/bruises/sprains

If a child is hit in an area it may bruise, swell, or sprain depending upon what they did to it. The best thing to do is get the child to sit or lay down comfortably. Elevate the injured area and apply a cool ice pack to help with swelling. Doing this for a few moments is better than not doing it at all. If the child continues with increasing in pain or the area continues to swell, contact an adult to let them access the situation.

I would hugely recommend taking a CPR and choking class. Your local fire department or hospital should offer these classes. You never know when that one time you could save a person's life by just knowing what to do in an emergency. These are valuable things to know. It will take a few hours out of your life, but well worth the time.

Week 4
Cleaning house

How to dust

Your goal when you are dusting items is to get rid of the dust. The best way to do that is with a microfiber cleaning cloth. Depending upon what I am cleaning, I have one for wood and one for non-wood items. I spray the cloth first with wood cleaner or window cleaner and then wipe the items down. The cloths will capture the dust.

If you have items with intricate carvings, use a clean-natural bristle paint brush to remove dust out of the tiny nooks and then wipe with a microfiber cloth.

When you are dusting, make sure to wipe around the entire object. If you are able to move it and wipe under it, then great. If not make sure to do all around it. If it is close to the floor, make sure to wipe along the bottom to remove any pet hair.

To help cut down on dust in your home, make sure to clean any furnace, dehumidifiers, or air conditioner filters at least once per month if not more. This will make them more efficient and also cut down on the flow of dust in your home.

How to clean windows

You can clean windows in one of two ways, by using a squeegee blade or with window cleaner and a microfiber cloth.

To clean with window cleaner and a microfiber cloth, just spray and wipe the window. If you are doing both sides of the window, wipe each side in a different direction to see where you have left the streaks at. I remember learning how to wipe windows with an old newspaper. It works great and does not leave any lint residue. Crumble it up and wipe as you would with a rag. Baby cloth diapers that have not been dried with fabric softener remove dirt and leave no streaks behind as well. But if you do not have these items, a microfiber cloth works great.

**Do not wash your microfiber cloths with fabric softener. They will leave a streak on your windows as you are washing.

If you have a squeegee blade, this is a fun tool to wipe windows with. If you are washing indoors, place a towel on the window ledge to catch drips. Using a sponge, wash the window with a solution of ½ vinegar and ½ warm water. Take the squeegee, wet the blade, then wipe from the upper corner of the window pane towards the bottom. Draw the squeegee down in a straight stroke. Return to the top and repeat, slightly overlapping the first stroke. After each stroke, wipe the squeegee off with a cloth. Finish by pulling the squeegee across the bottom of the window and dry the sill with a cloth.

How to clean a bathroom

I believe that every young man should need to know how to clean a bathroom. Bathrooms can be a relaxing peaceful place or they can be a smelly, disturbing place. The best way to get rid of odors in the bathroom is to remove the source of the smell. It doesn't work to just cover it up, by spraying chemically laden cleaners, and fresheners. Pinpoint the source and get it gone.

We will start with the sink. Take your all purpose cleaner, and spray it on the surface of the sink. Use your sponge and wipe down all areas of the sink. Pay careful attention to the knobs and the back of the sink, which can accumulate mold. Wipe the ledges and any walls near the sink. Toothpaste and soap can get splattered and hardened in this area. If your sink is dirtier and needs a deeper scrubbing, you can use something with a little grit. Use a scrubbing powder to remove grim from the sink. Sprinkle it on the bottom of a damp sink and scrub with your sponge. Rinse all areas down by wiping them with your sponge that has been rinsed in warm water.

Once a week you will need to take notice of the fronts of your sink cabinets. Spray some cleaner onto your sponge and do a thorough wiping of all of the fronts and knobs of your sink base. Continue around the entire thing, removing dirt and grime. Rinse your sponge as needed in the sink.

Wipe the mirrors and check them daily to remove any toothpaste or mess that is on them. If you have light fixtures, every 6 months clean them thoroughly.

Next, let's do the toilet. I can hear the cheers now ☺ I clean a toilet the old fashioned way, with a sponge or rag. I find that the brushes that some use in the bathroom, do nothing but collect bacteria. It is also one more thing that is sitting in your bathroom. It is really not a big deal, just wash your hands when you are finished, you will rid your hands of bacteria. I promise, you will be all right☺ Give the toilet a flush. Next sprinkle the toilet with the scrubbing powder and let set. Spray the toilet liberally with your all purpose cleaner. It is okay to get it on the rims and sides of the toilet, you will be wiping them off. Then you are to dive in. Start by taking your sponge and wipe the insides of the toilet in a circular motion. Do the visible areas, and then do under the lip of the toilet. Usually where the water level sits, bacteria forms at and below that. Wipe down inside of the tunnel, all around. Then give the toilet a flush. As it is flushing, swish your sponge to remove yuck off of it.

Spray the rim of the toilet and the bottom of the seat. Wipe the rim all the way around it. Continue down the sides of the toilet. If your toilet is extra dirty, squish out the sponge in the toilet water and re-spray the outsides of it. The water inside the toilet is clean now that you have cleaned it, so you can use it as a bucket. Wipe around all of the bends and crevices of the toilet. Wipe the seat and especially around the hinges. Rinse the sponge in between areas. Reapply more cleaner. Do the seat and then the tank of the toilet. Wipe the handle-as it is probably the dirtiest and oftentimes overlooked for cleaning. Rinse out your sponge again and spray the base of the toilet. Do all around the bottom where it attaches to the floor. Urine accumulates often down here. Do all around the back and the floor around the toilet. You are working downwards and outwards from your toilet. The dirtiest to the cleanest.

An area that doesn't usually get wiped is the walls around the toilet. Unfortunately this area gets dirty and can be a cause of smell. Especially if boys use this toilet☺ Spray and wipe it. Rinse the sponge afterwards so you can continue cleaning. Work away from the toilet and do the entire floor. Notice the baseboards and if they need wiping, do so. Wipe any lower walls that look dirty. Keep rinsing your sponge in the toilet to remove debris and grime. Continue spraying and wiping until the entire floor is cleaned.

Your bathroom is probably smelling and looking pretty great now. We unfortunately have one more area to clean---the bathtub. I like to take my powder cleaner and sprinkle liberally into the bottom of the tub. I add a little bit of water to make it damp and start scrubbing. I have a green pouf scrubbie that grabs grime better than a regular sponge. I do the entire bottom of the tub, and work up the sides. Move up around the ledges and remove any soap bottles and wipe underneath them. Work your way up the tub walls, paying careful attention to the corners and crevices. You can sprinkle the powder cleaner directly on your wet pouf. Do around the knobs and faucets as well. Take the shower head and rinse down the tub from top to bottom. When you think you are done, run your hand around the rim of the bottom of the tub. Do you feel any grime? Go back over that area.

Take note of your shower curtain. About once per month you should wash this. Put it in the washing machine with some heavy towels and that will help scrub the curtain. Hang it up wet to dry.

To finish, wipe the outside of the tub and any areas around it.

Look around at any walls that you did not wipe and wipe as needed. If you notice cobwebs on the ceiling, wipe them with a broom.

If you have a trash can in here, empty it regularly. If the inside is dirty, pick out the stuck on trash. Line it with a plastic grocery bag. It will make emptying it easier.

All right, you have done it. You completed probably the most dirtiest room in your home! I pray you did it with a cheerful "delightful" heart.

Remember to remove odors don't just cover them up, get directly to the source and get rid of them.

How to wash dishes

Some of you may just use the dishwasher, but washing them by hand is a much more efficient way to getting them done quickly. It takes only a few moments and will use less water.

The BEST time to do dishes, is IMMEDIATELY after they are dirty. If you leave dishes for a few hours or until the morning, the food is caked on and it makes it twice as hard to get them clean. It is best just to do them as soon as you are finished eating. It makes for a clean kitchen and then it is something you won't have to worry about because it is done.

1. Start by removing all foods and liquids from your dishes. Plug the sink, and start to fill with hot water. Squirt a few squirts of dish soap as it is filling up. The hotter the water, the better to remove bacteria.
2. Place your silverware in the bottom of the sink. Then your plates, bowls, and finally cups. If you have any casserole pans or pots, fill them with some soap, water and let them set next to the sink, while you are doing the other dishes. This will give them opportunity to soak and make clean up easier.
3. Begin by washing any glasses or cups. Wipe the inside and pay attention to the lip where the mouth touches. I like to wash with a microfiber dish cloth. I have switched from sponge to these because of the bacteria growth on the sponge after sitting out for days. Every night, I throw them into the wash and get a clean one out for the next day.   Rinse these in hot water, to remove all of the soap. Set to dry on the rack or towel.

4. Next move onto plates and bowls. Carefully wiping the entire object. Rinse thoroughly with hot water and set to dry on towel or rack.

5. The silverware is last, this allows it to soak for awhile as you are washing the other dishes. Don't just grab them out of the sink, wipe each item to make sure that you remove any food left on it. Rinse in hot water and set to dry.

6. Lastly wash and scrub serving bowls, pans and pots. I like to use my abrasive scrubber to get caked on foods off easily. If you have had your pan or pot soaking, it will help to remove the stuck on food much easier. What if you have food that is burned on the bottom, making it impossible to remove? Sprinkle some baking soda over a wet pan. Let it sit for about 15 minutes while you go about putting away the other dishes. Come back and start scrubbing with an abrasive pad or steel wool. If it comes off easily then great, if not, sprinkle it again and let it sit longer. I have had to let items sit overnight to remove some burned on turkey bacon.

7. Make sure and dry all items before putting them back in your cupboards. Wipe up any wetness from the countertop, hang up your towels to dry, and wipe up any water splashes on the sink. Check the front of your sink to remove any water that may have dripped down.

To cut down on the amount of dishes that I do have after each meal, I like to wash them as I am preparing them. This helps not to have an overwhelmingly full sink after a meal.

How to sweep floors

Floors can accumulate lots of dirt especially when you have a number of people walking all over them. The kitchen is usually a high-traffic area where food can get dropped and sometimes pushed in the corners. Sweeping a floor isn't too hard of a job. Usually it just takes practice at noticing that you forgot to sweep an area.

First thing that you do is to remove any rugs and objects off of the floor. Carefully pick up rugs and take them outside to shake. Don't shake them indoors, it will only make more of a mess.

Choose a broom that is comfortable for you, one that is light and not heavy. Angled type brooms work great for getting into corners and this is especially helpful in the kitchen. My favorite broom is a rubber broom. You can find these online and are fairly inexpensive. They pick up dust and hair more consistently than a regular broom.

Try and keep continuous contact with the floor, without pressing the broom strands down on the floor. Pay attention to corners and edges, where dirt can easily get left behind.

 Begin on a section away from your body and work towards your body, in a gentle sweeping motion. Some people like to work on the perimeter and end up in the center of the floor. Others, who have a larger area to sweep, might prefer to sweep from one side of the room to the other, by pulling the dirt with them. Whichever method you prefer, the more you do it, you will realize the most effective way to sweep.

Carefully sweep your pile of dirt into your dustpan and carry it to the trash. Be careful to avoid any overhead fans that may be on, to disrupt your dirt pile☺

To check for thoroughness, you can run a rag along the edges of your floors to see if you were effective at picking up all of the dirt. If you didn't, you may have to go back over that area again.

How to wash floors by hand

Why would you need to wash the floors by hand when you have all these great devices that allow you not to have to get down on the floor? The answer is simple....for the thoroughness of doing the job by hand.   For the most part, you can get away with doing this on a weekly basis, depending upon the traffic in your home

Even though we have many devices that do a good job of cleaning on a day to day basis, sometimes a more hands on approach is needed. When that dried, stuck on food won't move, a good hand scrub will do the job. Corners get dirty by pushing the dirt into them, that the pad cannot pick up. A sponge mop just pushes the dirt around. A microfiber one picks up the dirt better. But by using your hands and a good cloth, you can make sure that all of the dirt and caked on food gets wiped up.

Begin by having your floors swept. This eliminates the need to pick up so much dirt with your rag. Then grab a bucket filled with warm water and cleaner. I use a microfiber cloth and it eliminates the need to have to use any other tool to "scrub" the floor with.

A safety tip to remember is to make sure that no one will be walking on the floor If there are little ones in the home, get a fan so that the floor can dry quickly.

Start at your farthest away corner. Wring out your rag and begin wiping across the floor. It doesn't matter what "pattern" that you use. Just be consistent. Work from left to right, back to forward.

Make sure that you pay attention to the kick plate under your cabinets.

As your rag picks up more dirt, wring it out in the bucket and continue wiping. If you have overhead fans, I recommend turning them on. Continue working your way out of the room picking up any dirt in your rag as you go. Don't just push the dirt, pick it up in the rag. Think of scooping the dirt and grime from the floor into your cupped hand while wiping it.

Any stuck on food that won't get removed by the microfiber cloth can be done so with a flat spatula. Carefully scrape up the food and pick up with the cloth.

Dump the bucket into the toilet. This will prevent things from getting stuck in your sink drain. Make sure that the floor is thoroughly dry before walking on it.

Week 5
Sports and Recreation

Some of you may not be into sports and that is completely fine. There are a few things that you, as a man should learn how to do in your life. This will benefit your children one day as Dad shows them how to throw a ball and may let you be able to find a few more friends who have some of these similar interests in common.

Let's start out with a daily home workout. What if you don't have any special equipment to work out with? You don't need any. This is a beginner routine and designed for you to do at home. Remember you aren't going to see results right away. You will feel a bit sore but visible results can take up to a few months to see!

1. Chest/Triceps—start out with 3 sets of push -ups, as many as you can do, with 60 seconds rest between sets.
2. Back/Biceps—start out with 3 sets of pull-ups, or as many as you can do, with 60 seconds of rest between sets. If you don't have a pull up bar, look for a siblings swing set, maybe at a local park—where children are not playing, look around and you will find something.
3. Legs—do 3 sets of lunges, or as many as you can do, with 60 seconds rest between sets.
4. Abs—do 3 sets of crunches, 6-12 repetitions, with 60 seconds of rest between sets.

If you don't know how to do any of these, do a search online and find out the correct way to do them. Do every exercise slowly and with controlled form. For push-ups it means 2 seconds up and 2 seconds down. For pull-ups it means no swinging or kicking.

Do this beginner workout 3 times per week.

You also need to add cardio to your workout. Cardio means any activity—running, biking, swimming, walking, etc.-where your heart rate gets to about 200 beats per minute. How you check this is to feel your pulse and count how many times it beats in 15 seconds. Then multiply that number times 4. This will give you how many times it beats per minute. You need to keep your heart rate at this level for a minimum of 20-30 minutes.

Some other things for you to look up or ask an older guy in your life, to teach you how to do the following:

How to throw a football

How to shoot a basketball

How to kick a soccer ball

How to grip a two seam fastball

How to swing a golf club

How to putt

How to throw darts

How to hit a cue ball

How to pitch horseshoes

How to make the ultimate paper airplane

How to play chess

How to play checkers

How to play guitar—learn at least 3 cords "E,A, B7"

Learn how to fish

Take a hunter safety course

Learn how to fire a gun/cross bow/bow and arrow

Learn how to dance—each person will have different levels of what they believe is modest in dancing. Ask your Mom for some basic slow techniques—think waltz.

Learn how to swim or at least survive in water.

Learn how to type with more than 2 fingers☺

How to skip a stone

Take this list and search out someone to teach you how to do these. Mark off the list as you learn how to do them. Make it a goal over the next few years to learn most of them if not all. It will benefit you to be an "all-around" guy to know how to do some of them.

How to use basic tools

This is going to have to be more skills that you seek out from an older male in your life.

How to read a tape measure

How to swing a hammer

How to cut with a circular saw

How to use a drill

How to use a crowbar

How to use an adjustable wrench

How to use a level

How to use a solder iron

How to calculate square footage of a room---remember your math skills Area=length x width

Household repairs

Some of these you may be able to ask your mother how to do. These are all important things to learn how to do especially when you will be living on your own one day.

How to clear a clogged sink drain

How to turn off a toilet water line

How to unclog a toilet

How to reset a circuit breaker

How to find a stud in the wall

How to hang a picture

How to fix a small hole in the wall

How to fix a large hole in the wall

If you have the available tools at home, I would encourage you to complete a woodworking project. There are many easy beginner woodworking projects that you can search for online or at your local library through a beginner woodworking book. Find something that looks neat and easy and go for it!

Some suggestions from a school shop class:

- bread board
- step stool
- shelf

One thing that almost every young man and woman should learn is the proper way to screw something in. If you remember "Lefty, loosey, righty tighty" that will help you remember which way to turn screws, bolts, etc.

Cars and driving

One day you will be driving and have to know some basic skills. This again is going to come from an older adult in your life. I can type up step by step on how to do any of the skills this week, but it is only going to benefit you to actually do them☺ If you don't have someone to show you just yet, look online at some videos. There are plenty of step by step videos that will teach you all of these skills.

How to change a flat tire

How to jump a dead battery

How to check the oil in your car

How to parallel park

How to back up a trailer

How to shift a manual transmission

How to pump gas

Check wiper fluid

How to check your tire pressure—if you keep your tires inflated at the proper sizes it will cut down on the amount of gas that you spend and help your drive go smoother. Remember do not lose the little caps that go on your tires!

How to behave after an auto accident.

Let's pray that you will never be involved in this sort of situation, but if you are, it is best to be prepared.

- The first thing you need to do when you have been in an accident is to keep safety in mind. If you fear you have a head or neck injury, try to keep yourself stable. If you can get safely out of the vehicle to assess the property damages and check the other driver do so. If not, keep your seatbelt fastened, turn on your hazard lights, call 911, and wait for help to arrive.
- If you or the other driver or a passenger is in need of immediate medical attention, tell the 911 operator. If no one is injured, still call 911, tell them your location and tell them to send a police officer.
- If you can safely move your vehicle, clear it from the roadway so it does not block traffic. If you cannot, alert other drivers on the road by using your hazard lights, or warning triangles, if you have them.
- When speaking with a 911 operator, the police, or the other driver do not say that you caused the accident, even if you think you did. Do not apologize for the accident. The police report, witness statements, and scene of the accident will indicate the facts, so don't assume fault for an accident,

especially if you are still recovering from the shock of what happened.
- Use your cell phone to take photos of the accident scene, if you can do it safely. If there are any witnesses who stop, try and get their contact information so they can explain the accident to the insurance company if needed.

Some things to avoid doing after an accident:

- Don't freak out. Even though it is scary and confusing, getting super emotional does not help anything. Stay calm and dial 911.
- Don't apologize. By apologizing it is giving an admission of guilt, and can make settling the case more complicated.
- Don't stay in your vehicle. If you can get out safely from your car after an accident, do so. If it is a bad accident, you don't know that your car is the safest place to be. It is safer to be standing on the side of the road.
- Don't settle without proper authorities. It may be tempting to settle a minor car accident without calling the police or your insurance company but there are many reasons why that is not usually a good idea. For example, you may not be correctly addressing the damage, you may be legally obligated to call the police, and you may not be able to trust the other drive to pay as promised.
- Don't give out more personal information than is necessary. During the chaos of the event, you might accidentally give out too much information. This in turn could make you fall prey as victim to identity theft scam. The only information you need to exchange with the other driver is name, address, phone number, insurance information and vehicle information. Do not exchange financial information or your social security number.

How to behave during a police stop

- Know your rights. A police officer can pull you over for any traffic violation, no matter how minor. They can even follow you and wait for you to commit a traffic violation. Never fight with the police officer or act in a hostile manner, if you do they can arrest you.
- Look for a convenient spot to pull over. Slow down, put your turn signal on and pull over to the right. Try to find a close parking lot or wide shoulder of the road. Take the keys out of the ignition and place them on the dash
- If it is dark and you are alone, you have the right to drive to a well-lit area such as a gas station, before stopping. If you plan to drive until you find a safe place, dial 911. Let them know you are being pulled over and that you are driving until you find a well lit safe place to pull over. The operator will communicate this information to the police officer.
- Even though getting pulled over by a police officer is scary, you will be okay, even if you get a traffic ticket. Take a deep breath and remember that they are there to protect the well being of people.
- Roll down your driver's side window. Place your hands on the steering wheel where the officer can see them.
- Don't speak first. When they come to your car, they will usually ask for your license and registration. Keep your information in a small envelope in your glove compartment or clipped to your visor.
- If they give you a ticket and you do not believe you deserve it, do not argue. Instead, thank the officer and remain in control of your emotions. Try and remember the officers name for later and then you can take it to court.

Remember if you are driving and obeying the rules of the road to the best of your knowledge, you have no reason to fear police officers. Drive correctly and be glad they are out patrolling the roads to help prevent accidents, by other's not obeying the rules.

Week 6
All About Clothing

How to build a minimal wardrobe

Having a minimal wardrobe means a different thing to different people. Some would say you have 5 pairs of jeans and 10 tops. Others would say 3 pants and 7 tops. You are going to have to make a decision based on your lifestyle to what that means. You ultimately don't need tons of clothing to dress nicely. If you have a few basics and ones that can be interchangeable that is the key to a good wardrobe. Here are three things to consider when decided how many of each item to have are:

1. Keep clothes that you really like
2. Keep clothes that you actually wear
3. Keep clothes that work with different pieces to create different outfits

You have already learned about going through and organizing your clothing. You probably have already gone through most of your wardrobe. The key is finding what sort of clothing you like and then getting similar types of styles. If you really enjoy the comfort of one type of shirt, see if you can find other colors of the same style.

Two things that are important for a man to carry

A pocket knife or Swiss army knife—you never know what sort of thing you will ever have to cut open, screw tighter, or slice apart. This is a very handy tool for all men to carry with them.

Another item is a handkerchief. Now you may be saying, "What? That is old-fashioned!" Just as a woman will carry a purse with many items inside of it, guys are in need of things as well. I am sure you have run into that embarrassing situation where your forehead started sweating or your nose started running and you used your shirt sleeve, eeewww! How much easier to just grab it out and swipe your nose and put it away. It is much better than "sucking" up mucous. That is a very bad and inappropriate thing to do in public.

You treat a handkerchief as you would your underwear, throw it in the laundry each day after use. You can get a whole pack of these for very cheap. Maybe you have a sister who is handy with embroidery; she could embroider your initial on your handkerchiefs for a little style.

Tucking in your shirt

What shirts should you tuck and which ones to leave untucked?

- Undershirts—These can always be tucked, and should be.
- Polo shirts—These have an even hem and can be worn untucked. If you are going for a dressier look you can tuck them in.
- Hawaiian shirts—These and any other "loud print" shirts don't get tucked.
- T-shirts—Opinions are going to vary widely on this one. Some like the visible belt buckle, others think it looks nerdy. In

general, don't tuck the T-shirt unless it's a deliberate style statement.

- Any button up shirts—Any shirts that contain "tails"—an uneven hem needs to be tucked. If you are going for a casual look, you can leave them untucked.

How to tuck:

You should have a clean line. It is an imaginary line straight down the front of our body. This line goes from your chin to your crotch. A well tucked shirt should sit so that the shirt placket (the rectangle of fabric where the front buttons are located) lines up precisely with the fly of your trousers. Your belt buckle and trouser button should be centered neatly in that same line. A clean line divides your body cleanly and emphasizes symmetry.

How to shape a baseball hat.

Sometimes you may get a hat and it is a flat billed cap. How do you get it to conform to your head? Well there are various ways to do it. Some guys take hot showers with the hat on and just let it dry on their heads. Or you can soak it in hot water and then place on your head.

But if you are not into a wet head, you can take the "bill" and shape it with your hands. You will have to have a "feel" for the perfect curve. It may take a few days worth of frequent manipulation to make it look right. The only problem is that you may wind up with a sharp bend instead of a rounded U. You want a nice upside down U not a V. You also want to make sure that the curve is symmetrical.

Another easy way is to place it inside of a coffee mug overnight. This is no hassle and leaves a long-lasting, well-formed curve in your bill.

You can also wrap it around a soup can and secure with a rubber band. Leave overnight.

How to tie a tie

This may be one of those things that you look at an online video to learn how to do or find a book at the library that shows step by step instructions if you don't already have someone in your home that can show you how to do this properly. If you really can't get how to tie a tie, you can purchase clip on ties that have already been done properly. But with a few simple steps and practice, you should be able to get it.

1. Drape the tie around your neck. The wide end should extend about 12 inches below the narrow end of the tie. Cross the wide part of the tie over the narrow end.
2. Turn the wide end back underneath the narrow end.
3. Continue wrapping the wide end around the narrow end by bringing it across the front of the narrow end again.
4. Pull the wide end up and through the back of the loop, under the chin.
5. Hold the front of the tie with your index finger and bring the wide end down through the front knot. (Push wide side into loop made from crosses.)
6. Tighten the knot carefully to the gills by holding the narrow end and sliding the knot up. Center the knot.

Ironing your clothing

This is something that every young man should learn how to do. Most of the clothing out there is wrinkle free. You can place it in the dryer for a few moments, take it out before it dries, and smooth the article of clothing. Most of the time you will be wrinkle free. There will be some times when you will need to wear a dress shirt and dress pants that are wrinkled and you will want to learn how to iron them to make them wrinkle free. You don't want an unkempt appearance. It really only takes a few moments and makes all the difference in your appearance. This is another skill best learn from someone, maybe your mom or dad or an online video.

Learn how to press your dress shirt

1. **Iron the collar first.** This is the visible part of the shirt as it frames your face. Do the inside of the collar first and then the outside.
2. **Iron the cuffs.** Lay them out flat by unbuttoning them.
3. **Iron the shirt front.** Start with the side with the buttons. Never iron the buttons, work around them. If you have a pocket on the front, iron up the pocket not down.
4. **Iron the back of the shirt.** You can place the sleeve head into the square edge of the ironing board to make this easier. Do one half and then position the shirt on the other side and do the other half.
5. **Iron the sleeves.** Remember to make sure the fabric is flat and smooth before you apply the iron. Take each sleeve by the seam and lay the whole sleeve flat on the ironing board. Be sure to line up where any creases are.
6. **When finished hang up on a hanger.**

Learn how to press your pants

1. Check your iron and label of your pants to ensure that the temperature is correct for the right fabric. Turn it on. It only takes a few moments to heat up. If your pants are made of two different types of fabric, often called a blended fabric, choose the lowest setting of the two.

2. **Iron the linings of your pants**. Most dress pants have inside pocket linings. Although no one will see these, if they are wrinkly you may see them through your pants.

3. **Iron the waistband and top part of the pants.** Turn front pockets out and then press the iron on the top of the leg. Lift the iron up, reinsert the pocket and continue to press along the top of the pants, paying special attention to pleats. Move to the seat of the pants, and pull out the back pockets. Press these areas and then move up to the waistband. Finally move to the opposite front side of the pants, turning the pocket inside out and repeating the process.

4. **Now you are going to press your pants creases**. Mark the crease at the bottom. Lay the pant flat on the ironing board with the cuffs right at one end, waist dropped over the far end. The waist can hang off a bit if the board is short. Flip a pant leg up and off the board so that you are working with just one leg, lay it flat on the board. Look inside the cuff and find the two seams. Arrange the pants leg so that one inseam lies right on top of the other, dead center of the flat leg. With the inseams in the center, the edges of the pant leg are where you want to press the crease. Press down gently on each side of the leg. This should leave a visible crease at the cuff and an inch or two up the leg.

5. **Mark the crease at the top**. Find the same two vertical inseams and match them up, one on top of the other, just like

you did but this time at the top of the pants. Lay the top of the pant leg flat with the inseams centered. Use the iron and gently press a crease into place along the edge, about six inches down from the waistband. Don't press the crease all the way up to the waistband. The bottom of the pockets is a good place to stop.

6. **Press the front crease**. Now that you have the start and finish of the crease marks, it is just a matter of connecting the two dots. If the inseams are still set one atop of the other, the crease should be the very edge of the pant leg as it lies flat. Press gently down in one spot with the iron. Then lift the iron, move up a bit, and do it again. Work all the way up from the marker at the cuff to the marker just below the pockets.

7. **Press the back crease.** The back crease should be directly opposite the front crease. Repeat the same process you used to create the front crease.

8. **Press down the pant leg.** Once you have your creases set you can press down the center of the pant leg between the creases to get out any small wrinkles or folds. Use the same motion you have been using: press the iron flat, pick it back up, and repeat again a little further along.

9. **Repeat the other leg.**

10. **Iron the seat and front of pants as needed.**

How to fold a shirt.

1. **Lay the shirt flat, make sure it is buttoned up.**

2. **Fold the sleeves to the middle of the back**. Fold in each sleeve horizontally so that the cuffs cross over the middle of the back. Take care not to fold in the shirt's side seam.

3. **Fold the sides to the middle.** Fold in both sleeves again, this time brining the shirt's side seams in evenly from the shoulder to hem, so they meet under the collar, forming a broad V shape there. (The sides won't necessarily meet farther down the shirt.)

4. **Fold in half lengthwise.** Holding the bottom of the shirt with two hands, fold shirt in half lengthwise from the bottom up so that the bottom edge of the shirt rests below the bottom of the collar. Do this once or twice, depending on the length of the shirt and the depth of your storage space. Flip folded shirt over and store.

How to fold pants.

1. Hold pants by the waistband, give them a good flap to get a large portion of the wrinkles out.

2. Then put your hands in the both pockets and smooth them down.

3. Holding the pants by the waistband, fold them back on themselves—back pocket to back pocket.

4. Continue to hold the pants by the folded waistband with one hand and with your other hand, hold the pants by the crotch.

5. Now give them another good flap to get out the wrinkles and make folding easier.

6. Place them on your folding table and smooth flat with your hands.

7. Depending upon where you are storing them, you either fold in half or thirds.

8. While placing them on your shelf, to make them stack neater, alternate the waistband while stacking. This simple means to

turn every other waistband the opposite way. This will make your pile sturdy and look nicer on your shelf.

Your goal with folding is to create a square shape. It will fit in your drawer's easier and they will stack better when storing on a shelf.

Some other things to consider folding: underwear and socks. You don't just have to throw these in your drawers. You can fold these as you do your other articles of clothing. For socks, you place the matching pairs side by side and then wrap around each other.

How to shine your shoes.

1. Find an old towel to place over the area you will be working on.
2. Clean the dirt and the dust off the shoes with a brush or damp rag.
3. Cover the entire shoe with a generous amount of polish, using your shoe polish brush. Allow the polish to dry for about 15 minutes.
4. Brush the entire shoe vigorously using the shine brush. The point of this is to basically brush off all the excess polish, leaving only a small film on the outside of the shoe.
5. Then focus on the toe and heel for extra shine. Dip a cotton ball into water and squeeze out the excess moisture so it is damp. Then get a little polish on the damp cotton. Apply the polish on the toe and heel using small circular motions. This will take a while.

6. Repeat step 5 until you are satisfied with the level of shine. Use a new piece of cotton each time and to remove all excess polish before applying a new coat. The initial shine is the hardest, it should get easier each time you do it.

If your shoes have never been polished, your first time may take you awhile. The next time you do it, it will be less.

Laundry

Doing laundry is a necessary part of life. Even if your mother does the laundry, you should still learn how to do this for yourself one day.

To begin, sort your dirty laundry:

- Pile for towels, rags, washcloths
- Pile for bedding
- Pile for lights, whites, etc
- Pile for darks
- Pile for work clothes
- Pile for reds---these may "bleed" onto lighter fabrics

It sounds like a lot of piles doesn't it? Not everyone will have that many it depends upon their families needs. A generalized way is to sort your lights from your darks. Otherwise your lights will start looking dingy. If you have red clothing, sometimes the colors will bleed onto others. Check the labels for any new clothing as how to launder it.

You can throw a few towels with their respective piles (light or dark) if you have only a few to launder. If you have nicer item clothing like dress clothes, keep those separate from your work clothes.

To begin, put them in your washer. Make sure to evenly separate the clothing around the drum in the washer. If you put heavier items all on one side, it can make your washer off balance when spinning. Unroll pants and put them around the washer, instead of stuffing them in the same place. Do the same thing for bedding, wrap it around, instead of stuffing it into a ball.

Add your desired amount of soap. Check your labels. Typically you can wash everything in cold water. It saves on your utilities bill. The only item we washed in hot water was cloth diapers. We needed the hot water, to get rid of the bacteria. Skip the fabric softener, it is unnecessary. If you want a natural choice, use one cup of vinegar instead of commercial brands. Your clothing will not smell like vinegar when dried.

Make sure not to over fill your washer. The clothing needs to be able to move back and forth to wash it. If it is too stuffed or compacted it can't get clean.

Double check the settings for:

- Proper water fill
- Water temperature
- Wash settings—a regular wash is normally fine for everything

When it is done, you can take it out and put it into the dryer on a regular dry mode. For towels and beddings, a higher heat setting is needed. If you have access to a clothesline, hang out your items. Let the sun dry your items, its FREE. Be sure to hang just the ends over the rope, you want most of the item to blow freely to dry thoroughly.

Tips for hanging clothes on clothesline:

In the warmer months, this is a very effective way to cut back on your utility bills. By utilizing the "free" warm air outside, you can have dried clothes in a matter of hours. It sometimes takes some getting used to the stiffened clothing and towels, but if you think about how much you are saving---sometimes it is worth it. The stiffness will go away.

I recommend getting all of your washing done in the early morning hours ready in baskets to be hung out when the sun comes up. Take all of it out and begin hanging on the line. If you are going to be doing this much of the time, I recommend getting something to put your basket on top of so that you don't have to bend as much when getting clothing out. You can keep your clothespins in a utility bag as to not lose them. Typically, depending upon the humidity, your laundry should be dried by early afternoon and ready to be brought in and put away. I like to take like items off and set them in the baskets. That way when we put them away in each person's room basket, it is much easier than having to sort them. Towels we fold right from the line to the basket.

Here are some tips on how to hang clothing properly:

Jeans/pants/skirts

> Hang them by the waistline.

Shirts and blouses

> Hang them upside down by the side seams. If you hang them on the top by the shoulders you will have puckers from the clothespins when dried.

Sheets

Hang folded over the clothesline

Towels

Pinch one end and hook to line with clothespin. Take your next towel and let it overlap the first one just a tad and then hook that corner with a clothespin. You can do this for washcloths too. It saves on using up all your clothespins and the amount of time to remove each pin when dry. Just be careful how much you let overhang together.

Undergarments and socks

If you don't want the whole world seeing these, hang them on the back of the line or in the middle row. Hang socks by the toes. You can put a pair together.

How to get stains out

There is nothing worse, than having a stain get on your favorite shirt and then ruining it. Prevention is best, but obviously that is impossible at times, but knowing what to do comes next.

Know that if you put the item through the dryer or wash in hot water, the stain WILL set. Try and take care of it immediately. If you spill something on your clothing, take it off and rub a little bit of laundry soap and water on the area. If it is a heavier duty item, like jeans, you can use a small brush to help scrub away the stain.

The sun, is a great natural stain remover. If you scrubbed the area and it is still there a little, go hang it directly in the sunshine. Typically it will bleach out the stain.

Here is a handy chart for reference for certain stains:

Chewing gum Adhesive tape	Apply ice to harden surface, scrape with a dull knife.
Blood	Rinse in cold water. A squirt of peroxide will usually remove the blood with ease. Test an area first.
Crayons or candle wax	Scrape off with a dull knife. Place stain between 2 clean paper towels and press with a warm iron. Change towels frequently to absorb more wax and to avoid transferring stain.
Ink	Sponge the area with alcohol, rinse thoroughly then wash.
Any other stains	Apply detergent, or even dish soap with water and try and scrub it out. Dish soap will help remove any grease type stains.

Week 7
Cooking and food

Breakfast

Every person has to eat, thus every person should learn how to cook. I am sure that possibly one day you will be married and your wife may do the cooking. But one of the greatest things that you can surprise your wife or bride to be with is a meal made by you. You never know when she may not be feeling well or just might need a break. You can come in like a superhero and prepare this fantastic meal from scratch and she will be shocked☺ Or, think way into the future when Daddy can make spaghetti every Friday night or be able to make Taco Tuesdays. It will be a day that everyone looks forward to, especially by your wife.

Cooking is one of those invaluable tools that you WILL use one day in life. Yes you can get by eating processed foods. Your body will eventually let you know it is not going to function on them properly. Plus your wallet is going to benefit as well. It is cheaper to make meals from scratch instead of eating out or buying pre-packed ones. It really just takes a few simple steps and learning how to do them. If there is something you really enjoy, you can make a big batch of it and eat off it for a few days.

Instead of doing a step by step course in the kitchen, you can take our separate Kitchen Skills course to do that. We will just cover some basic meals so that you will know how to prepare a few simple meals from. Ask your family if it is okay for you to try out one or all of these recipes over the next few months for your family. The best way to learn how to do them is to DO IT! It takes trial and error in making meals. If you mess up, it's okay. Fix the mistake for the next time. Let's work on breakfast.

Breakfast has been called "the most important meal of the day." A healthy breakfast refuels your body and helps you function at your peak. Research shows that eating a healthy breakfast improves attention, concentration, academic achievement, and physical energy.

After a night of sleep, stomachs are empty and blood sugar is low. Start your day off right with a healthy, nutritious breakfast for optimum mental and physical wellness. A healthy breakfast should provide complex carbohydrates, protein and a little fat, because this combination will hold off hunger for hours.

Breakfast is the #1 most skipped meal of the day. There are many reasons people skip this meal. Most are excuses. They may sleep too late, not feel hungry in the morning, want to lose weight, or might not like the "traditional breakfast foods." Those are just "excuses." None are good reasons to skip breakfast.

If you tend to push the snooze button too often in the morning, there are things you can do to avoid running out of the house without breakfast. You can eat a banana, granola bar, or some peanut butter on toast while you are driving in the car.

No time to cook eggs in the morning?? Hard boil eggs. Then chop them up and set the mixture on a piece of toast with some shredded cheese. This is one of the easiest ways to get your protein in for the day.

Dieters rarely lose weight by skipping out on breakfast. By mid-morning they are usually starving, and will tend to overeat at the next meal. You are better off to eat a bowl of oatmeal or grab some fresh fruit like a banana.

If you do not feel like eating because you are not accustomed to it, force yourself to start with something. It may be as simple as a glass of milk or a banana. Then the next week add a muffin, bagel, or slice of toast. The following week try adding an egg or maybe some French toast. You will be surprised at how much better you feel when you do eat breakfast.

Planning and preparing a breakfast meal

The best way to become proficient at making meals in the kitchen is by actively doing it. Don't worry. Serve it at dinner time so that you are not rushed in the morning.

Things to think about:

- Try and choose a variety of colors for your meal. If all of your foods are white or tan in color, then the meal looks blah. Choose a variety of colors to also incorporate different nutrients into your meal.
- You want to try and choose from the different food groups when thinking about your meal. Keep it simple.
- Choose something from the bread/grain/cereal group—— oatmeal, pancakes, waffles, etc.
- Choose from your protein group—eggs, turkey bacon, turkey sausage, or peanut butter for your pancakes
- Choose some fruit —strawberries, blueberries, cantaloupe, or fresh pineapple.

How to make coffee in a coffee pot

1. Fill the carafe with water up to the desired amount of servings.
2. Pour into the top of the coffee maker. You can also look at the fill line and just pour water directly into that until the desired amount.
3. Place the carafe back on the burner.
4. Place a coffee filter in the top.
5. Scoop out the desired amount of scoops of coffee. If you don't have a coffee scooper, it is about one heaping Tablespoon for every 5-6 ounces of coffee. For a full pot (12 cups) I add 3-4 scoops of dried coffee into the brewer.
6. Close it down and press start. The coffee should begin brewing.

You will be able to tell when it is done brewing, whether your coffee is too weak or strong.

Add coffee creamer, sugar, or milk as desired to coffee.

How to make homemade pancakes from scratch

In a large mixing bowl add the following:

- 1 cup flour
- 1 tablespoon sugar
- 3 teaspoons baking powder
- ½ teaspoon salt

Stir together with a spoon. Then add the following:

- 1 egg
- ¾ cup milk
- 2 Tablespoons cooking oil—coconut, olive oil, canola oil or even melted butter

Stir all ingredients together until not lumpy. You can use a whisk or if you have an electric mixer, use that.

Heat your griddle or large frying pan over medium heat. Spray with non-stick cooking spray.

Use a measuring cup and scoop up about ¼ cup of mix and pour onto hot cooking surface. Wait until you start to see tiny bubbles appear all over the pancake. Lift the edge a bit and if it is easy to lift the pancake, do so and flip. Cook the other side. It only takes a few seconds on the second half.

Serve with syrup.

This recipe makes about 6 large pancakes. Depending upon your group you can double, triple or quadruple this recipe. If you want to be prepared for the future, you can mix up the dry ingredients and place a batch in a Ziploc bag. Seal it shut and write the wet ingredients to add to the mixture on the bag in permanent marker--- you will be ready for a quick meal when the need arises.

How to cook bacon

There are many ways that you can do this. An easy way is to just place in a chicken fryer pan (Think frying pan with sides) and place a lid on top. Lay the bacon next to each other in the pan. It is okay if they overlap a bit, because they will shrink up. Cook over medium heat and occasionally lift the lid and move around the bacon to fry it. It does make a mess and the grease can "pop" up and burn you so use caution. It is easiest to use a pair of tongs to lift the bacon and flip it over. When it is crispy and appears done, you can remove from the pan and it will have to drain to remove some fat so it isn't greasy. You can place some folded up paper towels on a plate. Place on top of the paper towels and blot some of the grease away.

Now your pan may have some leftover bacon grease in it. DO NOT pour this down your drain!!! It will harden as it cools and clog your pipes. If you let the pan cool you can just wipe it off in a paper towel and place in the trash. Or if you are careful you can carry it outside to dump on the ground. Some cooks like to save the bacon fat for other meals. It is a personal preference. Just DO NOT PUT IT DOWN THE DRAIN! As you wipe off most of the grease, just clean the pan with normal hot soapy water in the sink.

An easier way is to cook in the oven. For easy clean up, cover a cookie sheet with sides with aluminum foil. Separate the bacon and lay it in strips on the cookie sheet. You can lay them side by side as they will shrink as the cook. Place in oven and bake 400 degrees until no longer pink. They will get crispy. It is about 30 minutes. Check after 15-20 minutes to help gauge your time. Place on a paper towel to absorb some extra fat after cooking. Then wad up the aluminum foil---easy cleanup.

How to make scrambled eggs

This is an easy, protein packed breakfast to make.

In a mixing bowl add the following:

- 4 eggs
- ¼ cup milk
- a few dashes of salt and pepper

Use a fork or a whisk and whip the eggs until all combined. In a large nonstick skillet or frying pan, on medium heat , place about 2 Tablespoons of butter until melted.

Then pour in your egg mixture.

Using a spatula scraper, scrape the bottom of the pan carefully. The eggs are going to begin to set, gently pull the eggs across the pan with an inverted turner, forming large curds. Continue cooking by pulling, lifting, and folding eggs—until thickened and no visible liquid egg remains Do not stir constantly. Remove from heat. Serve.

If you want something special in your eggs, before you add the egg mixture you can chop up tiny pieces of onions, green peppers, ham lunchmeat, pepperoni, or just add bacon bits to the butter. Fry for a few minutes until they are soft. Then add your egg mixture. You can also sprinkle some shredded cheese on top or add a few slices of your favorite kind. The heat from the eggs will help it melt.

We enjoy serving our eggs with some salsa on top as a condiment.

You can serve these inside of a flour tortilla and make an easy breakfast burrito as well. There are many ways to use eggs.

How to make oatmeal on the stove

Bring to a rapid boil 1 3/4 cups of water in small pot. Rapid boil means when you start to see lots of bubbles coming up from the bottom of the pan. You can help speed up the process by placing a lid on the water as it boils. It traps the heat to help it boil quicker.

Slowly stir in 3/4 cup of oatmeal, 1/4 tsp salt, and 2 teaspoons honey or brown sugar. Remove from heat, cover and let sit for 1-3 minutes.

Pour into bowl and serve as is or you can add raisins, cranberries, cut up apple pieces, blueberries, or any type of fruit you enjoy.

Smoothie recipes

Using your blender to make smoothies is an easy and yummy way to make a quick meal or a special drink. Here are some rules for using the blender.

1. Always put the lid on securely when using. If you do not put it on, liquids might explode all over, making a mess.
2. We will be using cold liquids, but if you were to blend hot liquids, be sure to open the lid away from you to avoid any burns from steam.
3. Never place any utensil in the blender when on. Items can get caught in the blades and have drastic results.
4. Don't use a blender with a frayed cord. This could potentially be a fire hazard.
5. If your mixture is apperaring to not blend well, add some more liquid to help it.
6. When you are finished, place a small squirt of dish soap and about one cup of warm water into the blender. Put on the lid

and blend for about 45 seconds. Rinse the blender and let dry upside down on a towel. Normally you can unscrew the bottom of the blender to separate the blades from the canister. Be careful as the blades are extremely sharp.

Chocolate monkey milkshake
- 2 cups milk
- 1 ripe banana, cut into chunks
- 2 Tablespoons chocolate syrup
- 1 Tablespoon peanut butter
- 6 ice cubes or 2 scoops vanilla ice cream

Mix until well blended.

Strawberry banana smoothie
- ½ banana
- ½ cup plain yogurt or flavored if that is all you have
- 1 cup frozen strawberries or fresh
- ¼ cup orange juice
- drizzle of honey

Mix all until frothy, serve immediately.

Breakfast smoothie

- 1 cup strawberries
- 1 banana
- ½ cup oatmeal—uncooked oats
- 1 teaspoon honey
- ½ cup peanut butter
- 1 cup milk
- handful of ice cubes

Blend until well combined

Berry blast smoothie

- ½ cup yogurt
- ½ cup milk
- ½ cup frozen blueberries, mixed berries, or strawberries
- 2 teaspoons honey or sugar

Week 8
Cooking and food

Meals

I am not going to do a separate lunch/dinner because most people can make a dinner and serve leftovers for lunch the next day. This week is going to train you how to make a few simple meals that you can put together and make taste delicious.

You can choose any of the following recipes to make for a meal.

Tacos

1 -1 pound package of ground beef, ground chuck, ground round, or ground sirloin. The more expensive, the less fat and better taste. Typically you can use ground chuck.

1 package of taco seasoning

1- package taco shells—hard or soft shell

toppings—shredded lettuce, shredded cheese, salsa, sour cream. To make shredded lettuce, take your head of lettuce and slice it very thin strips.

Cook the hamburger in a skillet over medium heat. Use a fork and push the meat around to separate it and make sure that it is cooked thoroughly. Once it is no longer pink, sprinkle on the taco seasoning and add the amount of water called for on a package. Stir and let simmer for about 5 minutes over low heat.

To assemble, put meat on taco shell and top with toppings. Serve.

Pizza meatball subs

1 lb frozen precooked lean meatballs

1-15 oz can pizza sauce or spaghetti sauce if you don't have pizza sauce

1-4 oz can sliced mushrooms

provolone or mozzarella cheese--- shredded or sliced

4-sub rolls or hot dog buns

Dump the meatballs, sauce, and mushrooms into a large saucepan. Stir to coat the meatballs with the sauce. Cook over medium -low heat until the meatballs are heated through. It will be about 20 minutes. Stir it frequently. For each sub, place 3-4 meatballs with sauce on and top with cheese. You can serve as is or place it under your broiler in the oven to crisp the bun. To do this, place it on a cookie sheet, put in the oven, and turn on your broiler. Watch your subs as it will cook quickly and burn if you are not careful.

Sloppy joes and oven fries

1 lb ground beef, cooked as described in taco recipe

2 cans of sloppy joes sauce

1 package hamburger buns

Mix over low heat --hamburger and cans of sloppy joe. When heated put on buns and serve.

OVEN FRIES

You will need:

potatoes 1-2 per person

olive oil

salt, pepper

Wash and scrub potatoes. Slice into wedges. Place in bowl and coat with 1 Tablespoon of oil. Sprinkle on spices. Place on cookie sheet and bake at 400 degrees for about 20 minutes or until crispy.

You will need to know how to cook pasta for this next meal.

How to cook pasta

Fill a large pot 2/3 the way with hot water. If you use cold, it takes your stove that much more energy to heat it. Make sure that you don't under fill the pot, this will make your pasta sticky.

Turn the stove to high and heat water to a full boil stage. Keep a lid on the pot to conserve energy and to boil quicker. Some cooks add 1 T olive oil to prevent sticking of noodles and others add 1 teaspoon of salt to bring out the flavor. Neither are required.

After the water is boiling, add your box of pasta and stir. Make sure to scrap the bottom so that the pasta does not stick.

After water returns to a full boil, set the timer to the recommended cooking time from your box of pasta. You can turn down the stove just a little to prevent it from boiling over. Do not cover the pasta as the water will boil over. You can stir it during this cooking time.

When it nears time, use a slotted spoon and remove one noodle from the water. Be careful as this is hot!! Take a bite to taste doneness. If it is chewy, let it boil for a few more minutes.

When done, turn stove off and have your colander in the sink to drain. Pour the pot out away from you to prevent being burned by steam and dump noodles into colander. Use extra caution, because this is extremely hot and WILL burn you.

Shake out the extra water from the colander, and then return noodles to the pot. Do not put back on hot burner, or it will burn your noodles to the pan.

Do not rinse your noodles unless you are making a cold salad dish.

Immediately serve or cover with sauce. If the noodles are left to sit, they will get sticky. You can prevent this by lightly tossing in olive oil.

Mostaccioli or Goulash or Spaghetti

1 -16 oz package penne noodles, cooked according to directions or 1- 16 oz package elbow macaroni, cooked according to directions or 1- 16 oz package spaghetti noodles cooked according to directions.

1 -lb ground beef, cooked, according to taco recipe

1-14 oz can diced tomatoes with Italian seasoning or plain if you can't find them

1 jar of spaghetti sauce—any kind that looks good.

After your pasta is cooked and drained, place in large pot, add your cooked hamburger, add the diced tomatoes, and jar of spaghetti sauce. Mix and serve. You can top with Parmesan cheese or any leftover white cheese you may have.

You can make your own garlic toast easily. Use leftover hotdog, hamburger buns, or rolls. Spread butter on one side and sprinkle with dried garlic and parmesan cheese. Bake at 400 degrees until crispy.

Serve with a bag of salad and you have a complete meal.

Pasta is made up of the same ingredients. The above recipe is called spaghetti if you use spaghetti noodles, it is called goulash if you use the elbow macaroni and it is called mostaccioli if you use the penne pasta. All taste the same, just a different shaped noodle.

As you become better in the kitchen, you can make your own jarred spaghetti sauce. You begin with tomato sauce as your base. To this tomato sauce you add spices to turn it into a finalized sauce. We add the following:

- basil
- oregano
- minced garlic
- salt
- sugar
- minced onion

You begin by adding 1 teaspoon of each. Then you taste your sauce. You decide what you need more of......salt.....sweetness....then add another teaspoon, test it and decide. For the first few times, write down how much you add. As you make it more and more, you will come up with a perfected recipe.

Roast in the Crockpot

If you own a Crockpot, this can be something that you make in the morning and let it cook all day. It is an invaluable tool. Do not attempt to do this if you only have a few hours.

You will need:

- 1 can cream of mushroom soup
- 1 can condensed beef broth
- 1 enveloped onion soup mix
- 1-3 lb eye-of-round or chuck roast
- 1 teaspoon pepper
- 2-3 potatoes, scrubbed and cut into cubes
- a handful of baby carrots

Combine soup, broth, and soup mix in the crock pot and mix well. Place roast in crock pot. Put potatoes and carrots on top. Sprinkle with pepper. Cook, covered, on low for 8 hours or on medium for 6 hours.

Beef stroganoff

you will need the following:

- 1 pound lean round steak
- 1 Tablespoon butter
- 1 can cream of mushroom soup
- 1 can French onion soup
- 1 cup sour cream

Cut steak into strips. Melt butter in skillet. Add steak and cook on medium high until browned on both sides. Add soups. Bring to a simmer and simmer on low for 20 minutes, stirring occasionally.

Simmer means small bubbling.

Stir in sour cream and remove from heat. Serve over cooked pasta.

If you have leftover roast, you can use that in this recipe as well.

Chicken pot pie

You will need one prepackaged pie crust.

STEP ONE:

Heat oven to 350 degrees. Open up prepackaged pie crusts and unroll carefully. You are going to place one in a 9-inch glass pie pan and carefully mold it to the pan.

STEP TWO:
combine and mix the following in a bowl:

- 1 can cream of chicken soup
- 1 can mixed vegetables, drained
- 1 can chunk chicken breast, or 1 cup shredded chicken

STEP THREE
Spoon chicken mixture into crust-lined pan.

Carefully unroll second crust and lay over top of pie. Seal edges by pinching together. Cut slits in several places on top crust with a butter knife.

STEP FOUR:
Bake 45 to 60 minutes or until crust is golden brown.

Barbecued Beef Fajitas

1 tablespoon oil
1 pound beef sirloin steak, cut into strips
1 red pepper, cut into strips
1 green pepper, cut into strips
1 onion, halved, sliced
1/2 cup BBQ Sauce
8 small flour tortillas

Start by heating the oil in large skillet on medium-high heat. Add meat and cook for 3 minutes on each side. Add vegetables, cooking for 3-4 minutes or until the meat is done and the vegetables are crisp-tender, stirring frequently.

Stir in the barbecue sauce and cook on medium-low heat until it's heated through, stirring occasionally.

Spoon the mixture onto the tortillas and serve.

Week 9
Personal habits and outside work

One of the nicest things you can do to prepare yourself for your future bride, or just to help your mother out, is by learning to pick up after yourself and how to become self-sufficient. Even if you do not get married, learning how to be responsible in picking up after yourself is a good skill to have.

You don't enter a marriage with the presumptions that your wife should pick up after you. You should learn to be responsible to pick up after your own self. It shows manliness and strength. It takes a few extra seconds out of your day and will be a great blessing to your spouse.

Even if you don't intend on getting married, you are still going to have to know how to clean things up and take care of them. One thing that I have learned from having boys, is that they can get things clean once they set their minds to it. I don't usually have them do all the daily work that is indoors, but when I have a task that needs scrubbing, my boys will do a great job, it might not be up to "mom's standards" but I have seen them take rusty car parts back to shiny new original newness, I KNOW they can clean a shower from time to time.

Remember these personal habits:

1. When you take off your clothing, check your pockets before putting them in the laundry hamper. If you DO NOT check

your pockets—you will be in danger of destroying MP3 players, money will become lost, and paperwork ruined—by going through the washer. Don't assume that your mother or sister will check your pant pockets—BE RESPONSIBLE do this yourself.

2. Don't leave dirty laundry lying around, put it in the hamper.
3. When you wake up in the morning, immediately make your bed—this takes seconds and will make your room appear to be cleaner.
4. When you use the bathroom—wipe any mess that you may leave on the seat. I think this has been a continuing joke for women for years—but if you make a mess, wipe it up. If you can get in the habit of putting the toilet seat down—please do. You may have young children one day and an open toilet will lead to curious little ones.
5. In the shower, when you are finished, spray down the walls or wipe off any mess that you may have left.
6. When you brush your teeth or shave, wipe up your mess. Just as you would not want to have to wipe up someone's spit or tiny hairs—no one else enjoys it either.
7. When you are finished eating, take your dishes to the sink to be washed. Be sure your plate is cleaned off, scrape any leftover food scraps into the trash.
8. Everyone has their own rules about taking shoes off in the home—but NOT wearing shoes in the home, will help your floors last much longer through life. Get into the habit of taking off your shoes as soon as you come in the door.

Don't get into the habit of just setting your stuff down wherever you like. When you walk in the door, take the items to their place. Put trash in the waste basket, hang coats up, and put your wallet and keys in the same place each day. Have a designated place for all to ensure that you find it.

How to take out the trash

This might seem like a no brainer, but there are some tips that can help you take out the trash effectively:

- When emptying the cans indoors, make sure to wipe down any that are damp on the inside. Pick up any trash that might have fallen underneath the bag. This will keep bacteria from forming and prevent nasty trash smell.
- Keep the trash light. Don't over fill the bags, when you go to lift them out the bags will break and you will have a mess. Pay attention to how full the trash can is each day.
- When carrying the trash from the inside out, make sure that it is not dripping all over the floor. If it is, wipe it up immediately with some cleaner and a rag.
- When you place the trash outdoors in a larger can, put the lid on tightly. This will keep any animals or rain water that may enter the cans at bay.
- When you have windy days and things blow, make sure that your lids did not fly away. If they do, go look for them. Having a no lid trash can is NOT effective.
- When the garbage men take your trash, if you find your lids are blowing away—zip tie them to the handles. Make sure it isn't too tight to not be able to put the lid on.
- When you take the trash out—as you are walking to the road, look around your yard for any trash that you can pick up and add to your can.
- When you take the empty trash cans from the road back to the house, pick up any trash that may have gotten dropped by the garbage men. If you keep your cans nicely in bags and tied securely, you shouldn't have any problems.
- Be respectful to the garbage men. They don't want to have to lift super heavy cans, or ones that have open trash bags. If you have a lot of items to put out to the road, put them neatly stacked. Tie items together, help out the person who has to

lift them up. Put yourself in their position. (Golden rule-smile)

Outdoor work

There is usually an abundance of outdoor work that can be done. It takes some paying attention and motivation to get things started. Here is a simple way to begin:

- Do your work in a clockwise pattern.
- Start in the front of your yard, going around picking up any trash or sticks that can be picked up.
- Grab a rake and clean out any flower beds or areas that need to be raked up.
- Keep a wheelbarrow or trash can handy for picking up debris and yard mess.
- Work all the way around your yard. You will be surprised at all of the little things that get left around in the grass. Pay attention to look for any rocks—they will ruin your lawnmower as you cut the grass.
- If you have a dog, pick up any dog mess
- If your parents allow you to cut the grass, then do so. Make sure you know what you are doing before you begin. When you cut the grass, change up the way you cut it each time. You can do crisscross cutting–like a checkerboard. You can work in a circle–starting on the outside working your way to the center. Or you can go back and forth, overlapping rows as you walk. Whichever way you choose, use caution to watch out for any people, animals, or objects.
- When you are finished, hose off the lawnmower to remove any grass. Park it where it goes. If it needs a tarp, put that on securely. Put away gas containers or any other item you brought out.

- Take a broom and sweep off any walkways or porches. You made need to hose them off, depending upon how dirty they may be.
- Coil up any hoses to make them look neat.
- Put away any tools and wind up any cords that you used.
- Wash any windows on the outside. You can use window cleaner and a microfiber cloth. Some people recycle and use black and white newspaper to wipe them. It doesn't leave behind any lint. If the window sills are dirty, you can wipe them with a separate rag.
- Clean out sheds and garages on a weekly or monthly basis. Throw away old items and keep it organized and neat. Again, work in a clockwise pattern when cleaning these areas.

Every week you should take the responsibility and make sure that the vehicles in the home are clean. It is good to do this on Saturday, so that it is clean for church. This is a good step in showing responsibility for things.

Here are some tips for washing a car

- Use soap that is specifically made for washing cars. Using household soaps may strip off the protective wax on your vehicle.
- Apply the suds with a large, soft sponge or lamb's wool mitt.
- Use a separate sponge to clean the wheels and tires, which may be coated with sand, brake dust, and other debris which could mar the car's finish.   You can also use a special wheel cleaner that you spray on separately.
- Don't wash when the body is hot, such as after it has been driven or is parked in direct sunlight for awhile. Heat speeds up drying of soap and water, which will increase chances of spots while washing.

- Don't move sponge in circles, this will create light, but noticeable scratches. Instead, move lengthwise across the hood and other body panels.
- Do rinse all surfaces thoroughly with water before you begin with a new section. Wash and rinse each section. This will ensure you have plenty of time to rinse before the soap dries. Start at the top and work your way around the car.
- Don't let the car air dry, this will leave watermarks. Use a chamois or soft towel. Blot up the water instead of dragging it across the vehicle.

Here are some tips on how to clean the inside

- Pick up all trash and throw into a trash can. Remove all items that do not belong in the vehicle.
- Vacuum up the seats, carpets, and all nooks and crannies.
- Clean the mats. If you have material mats, you can use a spray on foam and then scrub off with a brush. This will keep them looking new. If you have material seats, you can do the same thing to keep them clean.
- You can use Armor All and spray on and wipe the dashboard and all hard surfaces. Make sure to wipe off thoroughly. If you have leather seats you can also wipe these off. Just be sure to wipe up as much excess as possible.
- If your floors are rubberized, you can use Armor all or Tire cleaner for the floors. After they are dirt free, spray on and wipe off. They may get slippery depending upon the texture so give warning to family members.
- Clean windows on the inside with window cleaner. Make sure not to get any Armor All on the windows as it will fog up when it encounters rain?!?!?
- Doing this more often cuts down on the amount of time it takes the first time.

Cleaning the dog house

If you have a dog, it is a good idea to clean out the doghouse at least once per month. Check for spider nests and be sure to remove them. If you have any other small animals, it is a good idea to clean out their areas as well.

Here are some tips to help you do a thorough job:

- Wear rubber gloves when you clean as you will most likely remove feces and urine from the bedding.
- First remove feces around the doghouse. It is counterproductive to clean the inside of the doghouse if you leave feces around, since your dog will track it into the doghouse later.
- Remove all toys' and place into a container of warm, soapy water and allow them to dry.
- Remove all bedding. You should always use disposable bedding, inside of the doghouse, as it may become wet with urine or feces, and water or mud. Remove all bedding and dispose of it.
- Sweep the structure of twigs, branches, leaves, and debris.
- Fill a large bucket with hot, soapy water. Using a stout brush, scour the entire doghouse, inside and out. Pay attention to the inside corners, as debris, feces, and urine easily collect in corners.
- Completely rinse out the structure from your garden house and use a hard spray.
- Disinfect the doghouse with a household disinfectant.
- While the doghouse air dries, clean the pet's toys.
- Inspect the doghouse to determine if you need to make any repairs.
- Replace fresh bedding once it has dried.

- Place toys on porch of doghouse.
- Never place food or water inside house, this draw rodents and pests.

Depending upon your yard you may have responsibilities in keeping the pool clean or maybe you help in the garden. Whatever the job, take the initiative and keep it maintained. Take pride in the things that you own. Don't make your parents have to remind you that the yard needs cleaning up, do it every night. Walk around your yard, putting away items that may have gotten left out. Going that extra mile, will make a huge difference in keeping things clean. Plus, sometimes other people will notice the job that you do. That could potentially be a job for you in helping a neighbor maintain their yards.

Week 10

Child care and safety

Babysitting

You may in the next few years get the opportunity to babysit young children. This may come easier for some, as you may be used to many little ones in your home, but for others it might be a new concept.   With a few essentials and a little knowledge you can be confident that you will be victorious if you are left with the task of watching little ones.

Managing little children can sometimes be a challenge. One moment they are snuggling up for stories and the next they are painting the walls purple! How do you deal and cope with that? You PLAN AHEAD for all kinds of possibilities.

Babysitting requires skills in creativity, adventure, and play. Those skills will be of no help if you do not know what to do when a child has a tumble off the swing set or you are not prepared for the realities of a two year old temper tantrum.

Have a plan

You want to begin planning before you actually get a babysitting job. The best way to spread the word is to family, friends, and neighbors until you get more experience watching little ones.

It is about your safety and comfort level as well as the children's. Find out if a job is right for you by asking careful questions about what the family expects.

Think about the ages of children you would like to care for. If you are not comfortable caring for an infant or one with special needs, don't take those kinds of jobs.

Do you know how to change a diaper? How to bathe a child? Learn these skills before you show up for your first day of work.

The most important and first priority in babysitting is to keep the children safe. Being a good babysitter means knowing how to handle everything from a splinter to a real emergency. Remember our lesson on basic first aid?

It is best to prepare for an event before it happens. It is unlikely that the child you will be watching will eat something poisonous. But knowing where to find the poison control number gives you a big peace of mind.

Something as simple as feeding a young child can be dangerous, if you are not prepared. Know which types of foods are choking hazards to young children. Where can you put young toddlers when you prepare the meal as to keep them safe? All good things to think about.

Parents love babysitters who help children have fun and learn-while still reinforcing rules and keeping discipline. Ask the children to show you their favorite toys.

Take the children outdoors if you can. Simple games like tag and hide and seek are great games to keep children active. Running around also will help tire little ones out so that they will nap and sleep well, which parents would probably appreciate.

Avoid any type of media. Skip television, unless you need to keep them occupied while you prepare a meal. Engage with them to avoid them being bored and wanting to play tablets and computers.

Know that children will challenge you, especially when you are the "new" sitter. Even though a child may try and fight rules, they actually need and thrive best on structure and boundaries. Find out what the rules are with the parents and stick with them. You may not agree with what the parents choose, but you need to abide. This will gain their trust and respect.

Here are 15 games that will help you keep children occupied for a time.

1. **I Spy.** Choose an object within view and using the phrase "I spy with my little eye, something ___" Provide a descriptive word about what you see and let the children guess what it is. Then let them pick something and you try to guess!
2. **Would You Rather.** You ask some random questions to each child. For example, "Would you rather have arms so long they hung to the ground or three legs?" Or, "Would you rather be a bird and fly the world, or a cat in someone's home?" Or, "Would you rather eat a chocolate covered ant or frog legs?" These questions can vary to the ages of the children you are watching.
3. **Rock, Paper, Scissors.** The rock is a balled fist. The paper is a flat palm. The scissors are the pointer and middle fingers sticking sideways. Rock beats scissors. Paper covers rock. Scissors cut paper. Simply say "Rock, Paper, Scissors...go" and everyone throws their choice into the center of the circle.
4. **Name That Tune.** One person chooses a well known song and hums the tune. The other players try to guess the song. The person that guesses gets to hum the next song.
5. **ABC game.** Choose a topic like songs, animals, names, etc. Then go through the alphabet and say a different name for

the topic that you chose. For example, the first person says Ant, second says Bee, third says Cow, etc, etc. There is a clapping rhythm part that you can learn to go with this. You take both hands while sitting and tap your legs two times, then clap two times, then snap your right hand, then your left, then say the word that begins with your letter. Repeat these motions and the next person then says their letter.

6. **Went To Market.** The first person starts, "I went to market and bought a _____." Say it's a cake. The next person lists what has been said before, and then adds something. "I went to market and bought a cake and a doll. Person three: "I went to market and bought a cake, doll, and a bat. See how far you can get in remembering the items.

7. **Simon says**. This game can be played anywhere, even in a car or other small space. One person is Simon and starts by saying, "Simon says, jump'" Everyone must then do the action. However, if Simon makes an action request without saying, "Simon says" to begin the request, anyone who does that action is out. The last person still playing in the end will be Simon for the next round.

8. **Play duck duck goose.** Have the children sit in a circle facing each other. Choose one child to walk around the circle. As they walk around the circle have them touch each child's head. As the child says "duck", he or she has to tap heads until they tap one head and say "goose" instead. The goose must get up and chase the duck around the circle. The duck has to try and run around the circle and sit in goose's spot. If the duck gets the goose's spot, then the goose becomes the duck. If the duck fails to get the spot first but is caught by the goose and tagged, the duck must be the duck again.

9. **Hide the _____.** We usually play this game and use a favorite toy to hide. You can say to the child if they are getting hotter (closer) or colder (farther) away from the object.

10. **Red light green light.** With enough room, this game can easily be played inside. One person is the traffic light at one end, and the other players are at the other end. When the traffic light

faces the group, he or she says, "Red light!" and everyone must freeze. The traffic light then turns his or her back and says, "Green light!" while the group tries to get as close to the traffic light as possible. The traffic light turns around quickly, again saying, "Red light!", and if anyone is spotted moving, they have to go back to the starting place. The first person to tag the traffic light wins and gets to be the next traffic light.

11. **Mother may I?** This game is set up in the same way as Red Light Green Light. One person in the group asks the person in the front, "Mother, may I take <insert number> steps forward?" The person at the front then says, "Yes, you may." or "No, you may not." You can vary your requests by including options such as taking baby steps, spinning steps, leaps or whatever creative steps they can come up with. Again, the first person to tag the "Mother" wins and is the next "Mother."

12. **Hot potato.** Players sit in a circle facing each other. You pass an object, maybe a rolled up clean sock, or stuffed animal and they pass it quickly to each other while you hum a tune. The person holding the object in their hands when you stop humming is out. Continue playing until there is only one person left. You don't have to hum a tune, you can just say "stop."

13. **Hand clapping games**. The first hand-clap game most people have played is Pat-a-Cake with their parents. Songs and patterns get much more complicated from there. Usually there are two people involved, doing a series of clap patterns on their own and each other's hands while singing or chanting a rhythmic song. There are many rhymes listed online, but if you can learn from someone else or see it in a video, that is best, so that you can get the notes of the song and the rhythm of the clapping.

14. This is actually a board game, but you can play a version of it with some paper and pen. Choose something to draw and let your children guess what it is you are drawing. Very simple.

Depending upon their ages, you can be simple and draw objects or be harder and choose songs, books, or videos.

15. If you were able to have access to a deck of cards this game is fairly easy. Shuffle the deck of cards up evenly among each child. At the same time each person puts down the top card from their deck. The person with the highest card wins those sets of cards. Continue doing this until your hands are empty. then reshuffle with the cards they won in the "war" and continue playing.

Choking hazards

Choking is a very real concern for young children. The size of a child's windpipe is about the diameter of a drinking straw. Knowing what to avoid is the key in prevention. Here is a common list of choking foods for young children:

- Hotdog cut into coin shapes
- Peanuts
- Popcorn
- Pretzel nuggets
- Whole grapes
- Raw vegetables
- Seeds
- Dried fruit
- Peanut butter in spoonfuls or with soft white bread
- Ice cubes
- Cheese cubes
- Candy, cough drops, gum, lollipops, jelly beans

Common household items:

- Balloons
- Marbles

- Coins
- Small bouncy balls
- Marker or pen caps
- Button type batteries
- Screws
- Rings

You can help prevent choking by cutting the child's food into small pieces. Cut hotdog rounds and grapes into quarters. Give small amounts to them while eating. Take note of what is in the area if you are watching little ones who may put things into their mouths. If they accidentally put something into their mouth and you can pull it out, do so. Be cautious not to push the object further down the throat. Tilt the child forward to help force it out. You will learn this if you take a CPR and choking course.

When you go babysit in someone else's home make sure you have the following information before the parents leave:

Know their contact numbers in case you need to get a hold of them.

Know the home address—if you have to call 911 you will need to know where they live☺

Know names and phones numbers of neighbors or nearest friend in case of emergency.

Know any allergies for the children.

The main goal to babysitting another child is to keep them happy (and safe). This comes with having some creative things to share. Learn how to make the coolest, fastest paper airplane. Do some internet research before you go and practice this. You can have paper airplane flying contest. This will occupy them for awhile.

If the parents don't mind, learn how to make homemade flubber. This would be a fun activity to do with older ones. Just be sure to keep it outside or on a table. Clean up any messes that occur.

Being prepared is the key to a successful, happy, positive babysitting job.

Week 11
Getting a job

In your life, you will probably have to venture out and get a job somewhere, unless your family owns a business and you work for them. But for the rest, you will have to know how to fill out an application and how to interview.

Most jobs will probably be basic beginner entry jobs. Even if it is a job at a local fast food restaurant, presentation is key. If you want to land the job, make yourself presentable, each time you go to the establishment. If you are going to be picking up an application, wear nice clothing. Think church dress up. Don't walk in with dirty work jeans and a t-shirts. Most every teen will do that, stand out and be different! Make it a point to comb your hair and make sure your face and hands are clean. If employers can see that you will take the time to look decent, they will realize that you will take the time to do a good job in their business.

Ask politely for an application to fill out. Thank them by looking the person in the eyes. Show attentiveness. Go home and fill out the application. Do it neatly. Make sure you have all your information beforehand so that you don't write down the wrong information for references, etc. Put it inside a manila folder to protect it from getting wrinkled. Take it back as soon as possible to show that you are eager for the position.

Tips for completing application:

- Write clearly and neatly, using black or blue ink
- Check for spelling and grammatical errors
- List your most recent job first—if any

- List your most recent education firs and any training classes you may have taken.
- References do not have to be professional—use your teachers or if you have volunteered use a contact from that. Ask before you put someone's name down.
- Don't forget to sign your application

Companies get a lot of applications from people. What is going to make yours stand out from theirs? You attach a letter of application.

Letter of application or cover letter

Your application letter should contain information about the position you are applying for (even if it is as simple as working at a fast food restaurant—key is you want to go above and beyond and stick out from other applicants.) It will also list your qualifications for the job. It should be properly organized, formatted, and spaced so it's readable and makes the best impression on the hiring manager.

Here are some tips to writing your job application letter:

- The length----a letter should be no more than one page long.
- The format----a letter should be single spaced with a double space between each paragraph. Use 1 inch margins and align your text to the left.
- The font---- traditional font such as Times New Roman or Calibri. The font size should be 10-12 points.

Begin with the header.

This should include the employer's contact information (name, address, phone number, email) followed by the date.

Then begin with Dear Mr./Ms. Last name. If you don't know the employer's last name, simply write, "Dear Hiring Manager"

Introduction. Begin by stating what job you are applying for. Explain where you heard about the job, particularly if you heard it from a contact associate.

Next paragraph: Briefly mention how your skills and experience match the position you are applying for.

Next paragraph: Explain why you are interested in the job and why you make an excellent candidate for the position. Mention specific qualifications listed in the job posting and explain how you meet those qualifications.

Closing: Restate how your skills make you a strong fit for the position. State you would like to interview and/or discuss employment opportunities. Thank them for their consideration in taking the time to review your application.

Signature: End with your signature, handwritten followed by your typed name, followed by your contact information.

Always proof and edit your letter. A simple mistake and your potential employer may just throw it away.

On the next page contains a sample letter. Customize it to your needs. It is just a sample.

Name
Title
Company
Address
City, State, Zip Code

(4 spaces)

Date

(2 spaces)

Dear Hiring Manager,

(2 spaces)

I am interested in the part-time position that you have offered in your horse stables advertised in The Times. I have equine experience as I have been around horses for over nine years.

Not only have I shown and ridden horses, but I have also had extensive experience assisting in a barn. Through working with horses, I have acquired a thorough knowledge of horses, tack, and equine apparel for both horse and rider.

While I have equine experience, I also have excellent communication skills and an aptitude for customer service. My past experience as a volunteer at Pardee Hospital made it necessary for me to focus on providing quality customer service, and also enabled me to work with all types of people. I believe that my communication skills, partnered with my equine knowledge, would make me an asset to your company

Thank you for your consideration. I can be reached at 111-111-1111 or yourname@email.com. I look forward to hearing from you soon.

Sincerely,

Your Signature *(hard copy letter)*

Your Typed Name

First Name Last Name
Address
City, State, Zip Code

Follow up and interview

After you have applied for a position, give it about a week and if you do not hear anything, you can make a call to the manger of the establishment. Give them your name, let them know that you have applied for "said" position, and that you were wondering if they have already filled that spot. This will give you an opportunity to know where you stand in applying for this job. This also gives the employer a chance to know that you are ambitious and are eager.

Interview

If you have been successful in your endeavors and have been giving the opportunity for an interview, here are some tips to help you:

- Arrive a few minutes before the scheduled interview. Do not be late for this!
- Dress up for the interview. No shorts, no tank tops. Look professional, even if you will be flipping burgers.
- No gum and no cell phone distractions.
- Keep eye contact at all times.
- Stay calm, take a deep breath if you are nervous.

Sample interview questions

Here is a list of some sample questions that your prospective employer might ask you. Most questions are going to be about what type of person you are and why you will be good for the position. I remember one of my interviews as a waitress and they asked me what three things I would take on a deserted island. The boss wanted to know what types of things I valued in life.

Tell me about yourself.

What is your greatest strength?

What is your greatest weakness?

How do you handle failure?

How will your greatest strength help you perform?

How do you handle success?

Do you work well with other people?

How do you handle stress and pressure?

How would you describe yourself?

Are you lucky?

Are you nice?

How do you view yourself? Whom do you compare yourself to?

What motivates you?

Are you a self motivator?

What are you passionate about?

What are your hobbies?

What has been the greatest disappointment in your life?

What are your pet peeves?

Describe your ideal boss?

Why should we hire you?

Why shouldn't we hire you?

What can you contribute to this company?

Why are you the best person for the job?

Practice answering these questions beforehand. You don't want to speak in a rehearsed tone, this is just to help you come up with good answers.

Thank the employer for their time before leaving.

If the employer chooses to ask you if you have any questions and you don't, a smart response would be, "Is there anything that you see on my application that would prevent me from getting this job?"

Follow up with a letter

Follow up with a nice handwritten letter thanking them for the opportunity to meet with them. You hope your answers were up to their expectation and if it isn't what they are looking for, thank them for the opportunity for experience in job interviews. Have a wonderful day, Sincerely your name.

If time goes on and the employer let you know that you did not receive the job, ask them if they would mind sharing with you what made them decide not to give you the position. Ask them to be honest, because you want to improve yourself for your next interview.

Critiquing is a great way to find out what it is you are doing wrong as to not repeat it next time. Don't question why they decided on that, just find out what you can improve upon for next time. If you are truly willing to improve your interview skills, this will be your biggest asset.

Resignation

If you come to the point in your job and you need to resign, give your employer at least two week's notice. Be honest about why you will be leaving and leave on a positive note. You want to be able to use this as a recommendation for future jobs if needed. Giving two weeks allows them the time to find a replacement for you. This is common courtesy.

How to keep the job

You got the job, now how do you go about keeping it? Diligence is key in holding the job. To be diligent means that you give special attention to the things that are expected of you. Here are some more tips to help you:

- Be responsible and be willing to take on more. People who are willing to take charge and know when to step in, get promotions.
- Whatever your job is, work hard. Do the best to your ability from day one to the last day.
- Be honest. There are many times in our lives when we could cheat on our time cards or do less than is expected without anybody.   When you work, you are really working for God. The Bible says, "Whatever you do, work at it with all your heart, as working for the Lord, not for men" (Colossians 3:23). Do what you think is right to reveal your true character.
- Learn everything you can about your job. The more you know about your job, the more valuable you will become.
- Don't let yourself be distracted by other things. Take care of personal things on your own time, not on work time.
- Be a valuable asset to your boss. Be punctual, cooperative, independent, enthusiastic, honest, and fun. If you do a good job and are easy to work with, that is valuable.

- Do your job and more. Do the little things that make you stand out from other's performance.
- Don't be a time waster. Complete your tasks with speed and accuracy.
- Always be on top of your profession. Learning is a lifelong process, stay on top of things and continue learning new ways of doing things.

Week 12
Finances

There is NOTHING more important than to learn to be smart about your finances. It starts when you are young. Learn to budget your money and STAY within your budget. Read about putting away money from each paycheck and learning to live WAY BELOW your paycheck. You don't want to be what the world will tell you to do—live paycheck to paycheck and with credit cards. You want to learn to be financial stable and free from owing any man anything.

If you are young and are able to stay at home, think about saving most of your paycheck so that you can purchase your home. You will be much better off in the long run if you can buy your home for cheap and fix it up by yourself. It may seem like a huge expense, but if you saved 1-3 years of your income, you should be able to pay cash for a fixer upper home. Then take the time to learn new skill sets by fixing it up. When the time comes and you are to get married, you will have a new house, PAID for to show your bride that you have been working diligently towards your future. Nothing will be more impressive. Plus not having that added expense in your life will be a HUGE blessing.

Do the same for your vehicle. Save up and pay cash for your vehicle. Actually pay cash for all of your purchases to avoid the trap of credit. It will only ruin you.

Personal finance

You can take entire courses on personal finances and learning how to budget your money. The one main point that you need to know and embed in your brain for your entire life is:

Do not spend more than you make!

If you start now when you are young and continue onward while you begin making more money, you will be financially stable. Most people get into this thought of, "I am making money I deserve to have new things!" Or they start hearing about the "buy now, pay later" campaign and get into the horrible scheme of credit card debt. If you learn to put some money away for an emergency savings and then how to budget your money you won't have to worry about falling victim to that scam. If you choose to live without all the frivolous things that your friends may be wasting their money on you will be far better off in your future. It might seem like a punishment, but if you can live like no one else will at this young age, you will live like no one else will as you get into your early twenties.

Avoid any type of purchases that require you to make payments. If you can pay cash for something up front, you will avoid interest and fees. When you use a credit card and "borrow" money from the company or pay on a payment plan to another company, you are paying them interest to "use" their money. How much better to save up and pay cash for the item to avoid any fees. It is much better to wait four months and save to pay cash for something verses paying for years on a payment plan.

Avoid the statement that you have to build your credit score so you need to take a payment. That is a myth that you can easily read about online as false. Companies just want you to pay for years on interest payments when if you just saved up for a year or two you could pay cash for your vehicle and then own it yourself. The problem with taking a car payment or a payment on an item is that generally you will still be paying for your purchase and the item will be already passed its new stage and in need of repairs. You will be stuck paying for your monthly payment and paying for repairs. "Cash on the barrel," is an old phrase that is a good one to live by.

It is not impossible to save up and buy a car. Buy cheap the first time. Take care of your car and continue to save the same amount each month. In a year's time you can sell your car and then take that money amount and the amount that you have been setting aside and buy a better car. You can continue to do this and within a few years have a really nice car all paid for.

Look for ways to buy things cheap. Even though all your friends might be buying things new at the mall, think second hand stores. You can buy some really great clothing options at a huge fraction of a price compared to store bought prices.

If you have to buy snacks or food, think to buy them in bulk or make your own. You can buy a large bag of chips and then separate into smaller bags to have individual snack bags at a fraction of the price.

For gifts, think of homemade gift ideas. If you do an internet search on inexpensive homemade gifts there are tons of great ideas. There are so many great ones that people will really enjoy. Most would appreciate a homemade gift over store bought any day.

Avoid the sales pitch. Just one television commercial or sales person at the store can make you feel that you "have" to have that product. Let me tell you that sales people work on commission. Commission means that they make money based on how many products they sell. They are going to tell you exactly what you want to hear, thus they will make money. Here are some tips to advertising advice:

- Decide what you need yourself by listening to what the advertiser is saying. Make a list of other things you could buy with the same money.
- Compare products. Don't just buy what is advertised.
- Shop around. Don't just go where the commercials tell you.
- Go for quality. Make sure that the product lives up to the advertiser's claims. I like to think for most things—buy once

and pay a little bit more money verses paying less and buying multiple times due to it not lasting.
- Look past the appeal of looking good or cool. Ask yourself what the product can really do for you.

Making a budget

One of the first things you do when you begin making money is to write out a budget. This works best when you begin having a steady flow of income. It is kind of hard to budget money when you only receive a small cash gift once or twice a year. Maybe your parents give you an allowance and that is something you can work with.

Tithe

Your first choice should be to put some aside for tithe. This is one of the best practices to put into place now when you are young. It's about giving God the first portion of what he has given to you and allowing Him to provide for your needs out of faith. It is a simple concept but one of the toughest to live out. I can give many personal testimonies of when we did not tithe each week and how financially broke we were from it. We would experience hardship after hardship and it seems that things always broke. When we started tithing on a regular basis and it became a part of "wanting" to do it, things didn't seem to break down as much, we actually accumulated a savings, and God had blessed us in numerous financial avenues. Our base pay did not change, actually life expenses got bigger, but we still came out on top and overflowing.

Here are some Bible verse to read further on tithing, I encourage you to read them and study further in depth.

- Malachi 3:8-10
- 2 Corinthians 9:7

- Proverbs 3:9
- Luke 21:1-4

Expenses

Your next thing to list will be your expenses. Do you have anything that you have to regularly pay for each month? Maybe you go out each week and spend money with friends. Whatever you normally do, write it down. If you have to buy clothes, personal care items, or any type of snacks, write that down too.

Savings

You should start thinking about some short and long term savings goals. You might have to begin thinking about saving for a vehicle. You need to think about how much you can put away each month towards this. You might want to put away money towards a short term goal like a cell phone purchase. Whatever the item, you need to plan ahead. You need to set aside a set amount each month to work towards that goal. If you want to buy it in three month's time, take the total cost and divide it by three. Find out how much to set aside and then pay for it with cash.

Income

Lastly write down what your total income is for the month.

The difference between income and expenses should be in the positive. If it is not, then you need to do some adjusting to your expenses. You want to minimize your spending so that you can put away more into your savings, to save for future purchases.

Interpreting paystubs

This is a basic looking check stub. Look at the picture to be able to define and understand what happens to the money that you earn at a job.

Let's start at the top. It has the companies name, your name, and the payroll ending date. This means that this is the last day that they were paying you for. Normally you will get your checks a week behind. You will get paid this Friday for last week's worth of work. The check number is for the company to know which check was issued to you. Your employee number is the number they assign to you in payroll. The amount is how much your check is for.

In the chart, the left hand side lists the earnings. It has the regular hours that you have worked. In this case the person earns $6 an hour times 20 equals 120.00. If you had overtime they would list it under the word regular. You generally get paid more for overtime. Current lists how much the current earnings is for and YTD means Year to date. This is the total amount of earnings that you have earned up till this point. That is your earnings. Now we take a look at your deductions.

Under taxes withheld, it lists the four taxes that every company is required to take out. It is based on your tax bracket and the number of exemptions you chose when filling out your W4 forms. You did this when you got hired in, probably with your parents help.   They take out for federal tax, state tax, Medicare, and social security. Federal pays the federal government. State goes to your state to pay for libraries, roads, etc. Medicare helps the elderly with medical care . Social security goes to a trust fund that pays monthly benefits to retirees and their families and to widowers and children of workers who have died. It also goes to a trust fund that pays benefits to people with disabilities and their families. Some employers will take out for local taxes as well if required.

Other deductions includes any extra deductions. This might be for meals, uniforms, equipment, etc.

You take your earnings(gross pay) and subtract your deductions. This is how much your net check is worth.

I am going to recommend a wonderful course Dave Ramsey's Total Money Makeover. Some churches do classes on this, you may be able to get the book at your local library, but to purchase it for the small amount is an invaluable resource. I have all my children go through his course. They have one specifically for teens as well. He gets you out of society's buy now pay later mentality and shows you that if you live like no one else now, you will live like no one else later---meaning you will live much grander later on.

He also lays out step by step how to retire a millionaire something you may not think about right now but if you will, you will be so much better off financially in the long run.

https://www.daveramsey.com/blog/how-teens-can-become-millionaires/

Week 13
Outdoor grilling

Part of being a man is knowing some outdoor activities that usually the men take care of. If you don't know already how to do this, I suggest you learn. Gain skill sets for your future.

How to light a charcoal fire with charcoal and lighter fluid

1. Arrange the coals into a neat mound. Piling the coals into a mound or pyramid will increase coal-to-coal contact and help the fire spread.
2. Add the lighter fluid to the pile of unlit coals and light immediately. Carefully squirt lighter fluid on the top and sides of the charcoal mound, following the lighter fluid directions. Light immediately after applying the fluid. Never squirt lighter fluid onto flaming or hot coals.
3. Coals are ready when covered with gray ash. After the fluid burns off, the edges of the coals will turn gray. As the coals continue to burn, the ash spreads to cover each brisquette. Once mostly covered in ash, the coals are ready to spread out and use. The entire process takes about 15 minutes.

You can purchase charcoal with the lighter fluid embedded inside the coals. All you have to do is arrange them in a pyramid style shape and light with a lighter or match.

How to light a gas/propane grill

1. Remove the grill cover and open up the grill.

2. Turn on the propane tank, located underneath the grill. Turn as far to the left as allowed.
3. Push the knob on the right hand side first in and turn. The burner should light. If it does not. Turn the knob back to the off position and try again. Sometimes it needs another "spark" to light.
4. Continue doing all burners working your way from right to left.
5. Turn down knobs to a medium setting and let cook for about 2 minutes before adding food.

If the burners do not light, maybe due to getting wet, you can easily light with a match. Carefully lift the grate and turn the knob on. Light near the striker with a long grill lighter. Do this for all of the burners.

How to make a Dakota hole fire

The Dakota fire hole is a great fire to make. It is completely underground! It has a low smoke output, no need to worry that smoke is blowing into your face, and it has a much safer feel then a traditional bon fire. For step by step instructions go to

http://plainandnotsoplain.com/how-to-make-a-dakota-fire-hole/

Making a Dakota Fire Hole is initially more labor intensive than simply building a fire on the surface of the ground. However the outlay in energy required to make a Dakota fire hole is more than offset by its efficient consumption of fuel; it greatly reduces the amount of firewood required to cook meals.

When making this fire hole, you want to take notice of which direction the wind is blowing. If it is blowing at an east to west movement, then you want your vent tube to be facing the east side.

1. Removing the dirt and digging your pit. To make a Dakota Fire Hole first remove a plug of soil about 12 inches in diameter and dig down one foot.
2. Making the Airway - Starting about one-foot away from the edge of the fire pit, dig a 6-inch diameter air tunnel at an angle so that it intersects with the base of the fire pit.
3. If you see your spade sticking through clear out the mess that has gotten into the fire pit.
4. Now that your hole is dug , let's make a fire.
5. Add some charcoal....we really like the kind with the lighter fluid already coated onto the coals.
6. Add a small amount of kindling.
7. Then light it up.
8. After your fire has been preheated you cook on this immediately.
9. Add an old oven rack to cover your fire and cook your items onto it.

How to make a bonfire

Fire needs fuel, oxygen and heat. If you hold a candle to a log, it will not light, but why? There is certainly enough fuel and there is air all around it, and I have heat, why isn't this working?   There are some people who understand this, yet still pile logs on top of each-other and stuff the whole thing to with newspaper, and wonder why the newspaper just smolders and goes out.

Two keys here: surface area, and airflow. To catch a flame (and especially a spark) you need as much surface area as possible for your flame to catch (which is why newspaper works so well.) But you also need air to be able to circulate and get to where the flame is. In a fire, cool air has to come in from the bottom to replace the hot air escaping from the top. Keep that in mind when building any fire.

A good tip is to blow on a fire that looks like it needs a little extra kick to get going really well. Do not think that this means that more blowing equals more fire. Almost everyone blows too hard and too quickly which just makes things worse. Blow at the *bottom* of the flames with a slow steady breath, you will hear a difference when the flames get that "turbo charge" you are looking for. You want to keep that slow stream going as long as possible, so regulate your breath.

The fuel with the most surface area to combustible material ratio is called tinder which ranges from clumps of tiny fibers which catch quickly to sticks no thicker than a blade of grass. Next is kindling which can be about as big as your thumb. When building a bonfire, what you are really interested in is fuel. This is what really burns for a long time, gives off a lot of heat, and provides the structure for the fire. Once you have fuel going, the fire is well established; you don't have to keep feeding it, it's certainly too late to move it, and you don't want to be poking and prodding it too much lest you do more damage than good. It is often a good idea to add pockets of kindling dispersed evenly in the fuel to help ensure that everything catches together.

Choosing a location

You need space. Depending on the size, a comfortable standing distance around a bonfire can be 50' away! Anything within that range will be very hot for an extended period of time. The leaves on any trees overhead *will* die. Even if the flames do not touch them, the superheated air will kill them. Make sure the car is moved out of the way, and there is nothing flammable within that range (including plant matter.) Air is not a stationary force in your fire either. The wind can wreak havoc on a poorly made structure, and carry sparks into that gas can you thought was put away "well enough." Keep track of the wind, and if it is very windy, give up or be prepared to spend all night tracking down unwanted island fires.

Also be aware that the heat of the fire penetrates into the ground and kills all the microbes necessary for other things to grow. There will be a bald spot where the fire was for a very, very long time. To help avoid this, you can lay down a tarp and cover it with lots and lots of dirt to shield the actual ground from some heat. The bigger your fire, the wider and thicker the dirt pile should be.

Keep a fire extinguisher or a water hose nearby in case of accidental spreading of fire.   Be aware that there may be restrictions on fires depending on where you live, and it is your responsibility to find that out.

Construction of bonfire

You can make many different "forms" of a fire. The tepee shape is common and gives off huge amounts of heat and light. Generally there is a tripod of strong, thick logs which provide the structure around which the other fuel is arranged. They must be stable themselves, and be locked together well at the top. If one goes down, everything goes with it. When stacking wood around it, try to keep an even distribution of weight and combustibility all around. A perfect tepee fire will burn up evenly and collapse *in* on itself. Leave at least one opening somewhere big enough to fit both your arms inside it to add more wood and for when you need to light it.

Inside this shell, add kindling and smaller fuel. The more wood you add inside, the bigger and hotter the fire, but remember to leave room for air. In the very center, stuff a big wad of tinder, and a pile of kindling around it. You want the middle to catch quickly and light all around the outer structure. Once you light it, there is no going back so make sure that it is going to stay up before you take the match out of the box.

Any type of fire that you light outside, make sure it is out before going to bed. You can extinguish the flames with some dirt or water.

Grilling foods

Grilling foods is an easy way to make a dinner. They key is to cook at a medium heat. Don't cook it too fast as it will burn quickly. This results in your outside being crispy while your inside is still raw. Cook slowly to cook the inside and then it will just char slightly on the outside.

How to grill chicken

It is ONE of the meats that you want to make sure you cook thoroughly to not get salmonella poisoning. The other is pork. I recommend parboiling them in a pot with water and some cut up onions beforehand. This works well especially if you are grilling drumsticks, thighs, or pieces that are thick. If you are grilling flat thin tenderloins, I recommend marinated them in a bag with a bottle of Italian dressing overnight. Lay these on your greased grill and cook until the center is no longer pink. These taste fabulous. Remember to throw away the meat marinade and do not use it for anything else.

**one more important rule about grilling food........When you bring out your raw meat on a platter, DO NOT put the cooked meat back on the same platter without washing it first. That can cross-contaminate bacteria and get your guests sick.

You can place a piece of foil on your grill grates to prevent your chicken from getting burned too quickly. Place chicken on top of the foil and let cook. Turn it occasionally. As it continues cooking the liquid it will get that "grilled" look on the outside. Always slice in the center to check the thickest part for doneness. Chicken should not have any blood dripping out or remain pink on the inside.

How to grill burgers

A few good tips to grilling burgers. Flip only one time during grill time. Don't over handle them. Do not squish them with a spatula. If you place them on your hot grill, let them grill until cooked and then flip over. You can cut a tiny slit in the middle and gently push down to see if they release a clear liquid instead of pink or bloody.

How to grill ribs

It is a good idea to parboil these in a big pot of water and cut up onions for about 30 minutes. This will help cut down on the grilling time and ensure that it is cooked properly. Pork and chicken are two foods that you have to make sure you cook to avoid sickness. Parboil means fill pot with water, place items in it, then cut up some onions— big chunks, and boil over medium heat. Drain off the liquid and place on grill. Grill for 15 minutes and flip. You can then add some BBQ sauce to the cooked side. Flip over and add to the other side. Keep at a low heat to let the BBQ sauce embed into the rib. Cut a slit into a thick part to test for doneness. If you do most of the cooking indoors it won't take that long.

How to grill steaks

Place on hot grill and let cook and char for about 10 minutes before flipping. Cook the other side for the same amount of time. Depending upon how you like to eat them...from rare to well done, will determine your grill time. Keep the heat at a medium rate. You don't want them to burn the entire time otherwise they will be charred and extra hard. Keep them at medium heat to slowly cook the inside. You can cut the thickest part of the middle to check for completion depending upon how you like your meat cooked.

Week 14
Outdoor survival

This is one of those skills that will prove invaluable. There are tons of TV shows that deal with surviving in the wilderness. You can watch a few episodes and learn many great resources to surviving on our planet without modern day devices. The key to surviving in the wilderness is preparation. You can stockpile food and prepare for disasters at home (which are both good ideas—at least 72 hours worth of supplies) but the best way is to know what to do when you don't have the convenience of things or those things run out.

I would recommend taking a night and choosing to camp outdoors. If you can't go away anywhere, do it in your backyard. I know I have read about teenage boys who used their survival skills and camped out during the winter time. Take it to whatever extreme you can handle. One of the worst things in life is being unprepared and being unable to handle any situation that you are faced with. What if suddenly you had to find food off the land? How would you drink water safely? What would you do for heat? How would you be able to tell where you were at? All these are real questions that you should learn how to answer. There are tons of survival shows on television that you can glean from. The internet is full of different ideas as well. If you don't have access to either of those, the library has great books on survival skills for boys.

Some things to help you if disaster strikes:

1. Immediate security: If the building is on fire, get out. If someone is shooting at you, move to cover. Whatever the immediate danger, get away from it.
2. First aid: Attend to any medical problems that may have happened in the original event. Check yourself for injuries and treat them.
3. Self protection: If you are at risk from predators, two legged or four legged, you must arm yourself. This might be a sharpened stick, a knife, machete, or shotgun.
4. Physical needs: Shelter, fire, water, food, and hygiene.
5. Staying emotionally positive. When dangerous and depressing situations come up, be positive in them. Any doctor or psychiatrist is going to agree with this one. Know who your ultimate care taker is and trust that with his leading, you will be safe.
6. If you are lost, the key is to stay put as much as possible. If you are with another person or group, always stay together. Do not separate, and never move out of sight or hearing of each other.   When you are noticed missing, others will start to search for you. All you have to do is stay put and rescue will find you.

First aid

We have already talked about first aid basics in week 3. Some other important things to know if you can't get to a doctor or hospital are the following: **Remember to seek the help of a professional first. This is for if there is NO OTHER possible solution available**.

- Dislocated shoulder—roll on the ground or hit it against a hard surface to reset the bone.
- Dislocated kneecaps-stretch your leg out and force it back into the socket.
- Fractures—create a splint out of materials. A couple of sticks stabilized around the fractured bone and tied with shoelaces to hold the brace in place will help.

Burns

Remove any clothing and find lukewarm water to run over the burn or coat in honey if it is available. Wrap the burn loosely in wet clothing. Keep the wound elevated whenever possible and do not open any blisters that may have formed.

Dangerous prey

A simple approach when approached by wolves, coyotes, and cougars: face the animal and slowly back away from it. Don't play dead, run, or approach the animal. If you are cornered, make yourself as big as possible. Spread your arms and make a lot of noise. If this still doesn't work, throw anything you can find at the animal.

Building a shelter and start a fire

In order to survive you need to maintain your body temperature. This means keeping warm, but you also need to know how to keep cool if you are caught in the desert. A shelter only needs to meet two requirements: it has to block the elements and insulate for warmth. You can look online at an example of an A-frame shelter. It is simplest to build and will get you out of snow, rain, or sun.

Your shelter can be as simple as sitting under the overhanging branches of a large tree or rock outcrop. Beneath the branches of a large evergreen there is often a clear dry area, even in heavy snow. Avoid sitting on the bare ground or snow. Sit or lay on gathered small branches or shrubbery or on a downed tree for insulation.

A large garbage bag is very effective, inexpensive and compact personal emergency shelter or poncho that will fit in your pocket. Always carry one or two when you go off into the wilderness. Use the garbage bag to cover yourself and to keep heat in and the weather out.

To use, hold the bag upside down and go to one of the corners (a bottom corner, but now on top as you hold it), drop down about eight inches along the crease, and cut or tear a slit or hole only big enough for your face. Pull the bag over your body so that the corner rests on top of your head and your face sticks through the hole. Be sure to keep your head out where you can breath, you can suffocate inside the plastic if it covers your mouth and nose. If you have another bag and you're tall enough so one bag won't cover you completely, pull the other bag up from your feet. If you can, stuff the bags and your clothing with dry leaves for added insulation, but be careful not to introduce any unwelcome pests into your improvised shelter.

You can also use the bag as a small shade tarp, if the sun is a problem. A cap or hat is always useful to keep your head drier, and warm or shaded, as appropriate.

Use a tree, downed tree or piled up snow to break any wind. Curl into a tight ball to conserve heat. If there is more than one person, huddle together for warmth. In hot sunny weather, seek shade. If the ground is soft and you can do so without overexerting yourself and wasting precious water, scoop out a hollow in the shade, it can be 30 degrees cooler 12 inches below the surface. Once you have shelter, stay there. If you've taken shelter where it might be hard for anyone to see you, try to leave some sign or marker, sticks or some rocks, out in the open pointing to your shelter.

Attract attention

The more you can do to attract attention to yourself, the quicker someone will find you. The way to do this is by making lots of noise and by making yourself easy to see. You can be hard to see when wearing dark clothing, so it's always a good idea to wear bright colors when you go out. If you hear a helicopter, lie down in a clear dry space to make the biggest possible target for them to see.

If you are rested, feel up to it and there is a clearing, make a big "X" or "SOS" in the dirt or snow using your feet or a stick to scrape the dirt or stomp the snow down, broken branches and shrubs or rocks. Contrast and size are the keys to effective ground signals. If there is enough room, the letters should be 12 feet tall with lines at least two feet wide.

If you have something to use as a flag (an excellent reason to carry a brightly colored bandanna with you, it also has many other uses), that will be far more effective than your arms and hands alone. If you must use your hands alone, always wave wildly with both hands in an emergency situation. You don't want to be mistaken for somebody just giving a friendly wave.

Most survivors are found by ground search teams and a whistle is the most effective signaling device. A whistle is far superior to shouting because your voice just doesn't carry very far, especially in the woods. The whistle will be heard for 1/2 to 2 miles or even more in the wilderness where your voice may only carry for a few hundred feet, at best. You will also be able to signal for much longer periods of time, whereas your vocal cords will give out very quickly. You should never leave home without a whistle hung around your neck.

The shrill and unmistakable blast of a whistle repeated three times is a universal signal for help and will definitely attract the attention of anyone within earshot. Blow three clear blasts, pausing for a few seconds between each, then wait for five minutes and repeat until you are rescued. If you hear a whistle, respond immediately with three blasts every time. If you don't have a whistle, you can make a loud signal by banging two rocks together or beating on a dead tree with a stick or rock (but, be careful you don't hurt yourself or that the tree or branches don't fall on you if it is still standing).

At night, your greatest fear is likely the result of an overactive imagination fed by the TV and movies you have seen. While the sounds of the wilderness at night may be unfamiliar, there's nothing out there that has any in interest in harming you. If you think you hear an animal nearby, yell, make lots of noise or blow your whistle. If it's an animal, it will run off. If the noise is searchers, you have been found.

How to start a fire

When you are starting a fire keep in mind the wind direction and the surrounding area. A fire is important but you don't want to catch the entire forest on fire to attract the attention of rescuers. Build away from overhanging branches, rotten stumps, logs, dry grass, and leaves.

Look online how to start a fire with a pair of glasses or a bottle of water. You focus the sun's rays through the lens or water bottle so that it creates a single point of heat. Eventually it will catch fire.

It is also a good idea to carry a magnesium stick with you to start a fire. These are inexpensive and you can carry one with you always.

How to find water

In many parts of the country, you can find water by following the sound of a flowing river, but this is not always possible. Here are some tips to help you find water:

- Grazing animals usually head to water near dawn and dusk. Following them can often lead you to water.
- Flies and mosquitoes tend to stay around water.
- Stagnant water is not usually suitable to drink even if you boil it.
- Once you find water, bring it to a boil if possible. Even the cleanest of mountain streams have microbes and parasites in them. If boiling isn't an option, search out water from a flowing stream.

No matter how hungry you are, water is more important to your survival.

Sources of food to eat

- Acorn from oak: The entire nut is edible and they are easy to stockpile.
- Pine: The nuts and inner bark of the tree are edible. You can also make pine needle tea.
- Cattail: This is one of the best options out there. The base stalk is like celery, the root and tuber can make flour, and the pollen is very healthy.
- Grass: The corm, also known as the base, is starchy, but edible and filled with water and carbohydrates.

Remember some basic directions. Remember that the sun sets in the west and rises in the east.

A good recommendation is to check out some survival books from your local library and put them to use. Invite a friend over and camp out in the backyard. Learn how to survive with the basic items.

Things to carry every time you head out into the wilderness:

- Identification and/ or medical alert tag or bracelet
- A loud whistle—place it on a lanyard around your neck so it can't be lost.
- 1-2 garbage bags, these will fit in your pocket.
- 1-2 canteens of water
- a pocket flashlight
- a brightly colored bandanna
- a pocket knife
- fire starter (matches, lighter or flint and steel)

A good thing to gather and have on hand is a survival kit. This should be small enough for you to be able to carry easily. It should be water repellent or waterproof. Easy to carry or attach to your body and durable.

Inside you should have:

- first aid items-butterfly sutures, chapstick, needle and thread, knife

- water purification tablets or drops—you can also get a drinking straw which filters out the water as you drink—a good gift idea.
- fire starting equipment—lighter, metal match, waterproof matches
- signaling items-signaling mirror, wrist compass
- food procurement items-fish and snare line, fishhooks
- shelter items-snare wire, solar blanket

If you find that you really enjoy the outdoors you can ask for many of these items as gifts for birthday and Christmas☺

Week 15
Unspoken language

What message am I sending?

Without saying a word, we are sending silent messages to the people around us every day. Our face, posture, and every mannerism communicates volumes of what type of person we are. Being aware of what you do is a key to changing the way that others perceive you.

Your face

Everyone has facial expressions that represent our current condition. These expressions usually happen automatically. We do not consciously say to our brain or our face to show that we are surprised. We as human beings just naturally show these responses. Many think that we have a face that no one can read our thoughts or feelings. Often times that is not the case. Whether we have a raised eyebrow, a wink, a nod, or a quick frown it is likely we have facial expressions that speak to others. You need to ask yourself if your facial expressions are saying good, positive things about you. Are they showing the messages that you intend to show? The best thing you can do is to smile. A genuine smile. Nothing brightens a dull mood then a hearty, healthy smile.

Our posture and walking

 Having your shoulders slouch and head down are visual cues that you have a lack of confidence. If you stand with your head up and back straight, it shows that you have confidence and energy about you. It shows that you are a more approachable person as well☺

Mannerisms and gestures

You may know that folded arms send a closed message while arms at our side send an open message to others. Twisting hair, frequent facial touches, wringing hands, or scratching of the head may reflect angst. Many people speak with their hands and body. It adds expressive quality to their words. When you say the word, "no" while strongly pointing your finger makes the sentence more powerful. When you shrug your shoulders, it shows a lack of knowledge or interest in things.

Your clothing, hair, and personal care can send messages to people as well. If your clothing is wrinkled and unclean, it will send a negative message to others. If you have an odor about you, people will be quick to judge. If you are in a situation which you value, consider your appearance.

First impressions

Even if we think people shouldn't judge a situation, most people judge a first impression about you. I know for myself, numerous times I have met someone and had a judgment about them, that later I have changed. I was wrong to think that way, but it was how those people presented themselves is how I was turned off. Consider everything about what type of message you are conveying to others if you want to make it positive.

If you honestly want to know how others perceive you, ask a close friend or family member. Ask them if you are offensive or if there is anything about what you do that turns them off. Look in the mirror and see what others see about you. Take note of how you respond when faced with negative information. In times of stress, how are you looking? You have to be aware that others are watching you all the time. Especially if you have made the decision to follow Christ. They want to see what it is about this Jesus person that makes you so adamant about following Him. Make your life reflect how Jesus would respond in all situations. People are watching. Your siblings are watching, younger boys are watching you, and you are an example to those around you, even if you don't want to be.

Opportunities to serve

At church

Among your church groups, you may feel too old to be part of the youth group anymore but still not quite old enough to be part of the men's group in your church. I would encourage you to attend these men's meetings and gain insight and knowledge from them. They were all once young like yourself and you could gain much wisdom. It may seem weird at first, but give it a try. You can also see if you can help out in a younger age program at your church. If you enjoy working with children, try the children's church part of your church. I am sure they would love an "energetic" young person to come help with the children. . Everyone loves a cheerful, willing helper. Make yourself available, volunteer for things needed in the church. Ask your pastor to see which types of things you can get involved in helping doing. It might be as simple as doing yard work at the church once per week.   There is always something to do and probably not enough people to help do it. If your church is small and your parent's approve, search out larger churches in your area with young adult groups.

In the community:

There may be plenty of things to volunteer doing in your own community. If you enjoy working with the elderly, contact a local nursing home and see what types of opportunities you can have to volunteer. Your local library probably would enjoy some extra hands, plus you can gain some extra skills. If you enjoy serving others, look at your local hospital for volunteer service opportunities. Local animal shelters would probably have many needs for helping. Soup kitchens and food banks would offer positions to come help each week as well.

In the home:

I know what a blessing it can be to have an extra hand to help me out during the day. Be a willing helper to your mom each day. Set aside extra time to help school younger ones, give your mom a break, or help make a meal. Yes, this is true for young men as well as young women. If it is not something you are great at, then take on the role that your father would do. Make sure that you do all of the yard work, keep the porches clean, the vehicles clean, take the trash out, and take care of the animals. Don't expect your mother to do it, you take the initiative and do the work as your father would do.

If you do not have many opportunities in the home, look for another family whom you can bless. Offer to help a single or elderly woman with some jobs that typical males do in the home. Do not expect money, actually deny it. Take the skills that you gain from doing it and use them for the future.

Personal safety tips

As you get out more in the world be careful of what you encounter. Being at home most of the time is a safe zone. Being out in the world with ungodly people, gives you an opportunity to reach out to others and be a light. It can also be a trap for a young person, being out in the world for the first time. Guard yourself, take what your parents have taught you and follow it. You don't need to be fearful of things, but be aware.   Women are generally the target but young male adults are as well for random acts of violence because they generally have:

1. **Lack of awareness**—you need to know where you are and what is going on around you.
2. **Body language**—keep your head up, stand straight up.
3. **Wrong place, wrong time**—don't walk alone in an alley or drive in a bad neighborhood at night.

Here is a list of basic tips to remember:

- Never be alone with another woman, no matter what the age—in work situations, in vehicles, etc. It is just not a proper situation to put yourself or the woman into. This would be a wise choice to remain pure.
- Unfortunately our world is full of immodesty. You see it while walking at the mall, when walking down the road, and sometimes even in churches. Train your eyes to always look down when passing by suspecting targets. You want to guard your eyes from that sort of lust. It is just temptation and should be avoided.
- Treat all women or girls with respect. Be chivalrous in your actions to them. Hold a high standard towards them
- Don't make your life dependent upon a woman. Some guys will require mom to do all the work, then they leave home, are bachelors, and are slobs. Set a standard for yourself and learn to be self sufficient. You don't get married to have your wife pick up after you. You get married to share a life with someone.
- Have control over your emotions. Learn to control your anger and jealousy if any. A man who has no control over these emotions, will not show himself worthy to someone. If you can learn to control your anger, it shows a lot about your character and what type of man you are.

Take this week and make a list of goals for yourself in life. This gives you something to look forward to and to work towards. If you don't know where you are going, how are you going to get there? Or even know when you get there?

My educational goals include:

1. _____
_____
_____

2. _____
_____
_____

3. _____
_____
_____

4. _____
_____
_____

5. _____
_____
_____

My social goals include:

1. _____
_____

2. _____
_____

3. _____
_____

4. _____
_____

5. _____
_____
_____

My financial goals:

1. _____
   _____

2. _____
   _____

3. _____
   _____

4. _____
   _____

5. _____
   _____
   _____

My family goals include:

1. _____
   _____

2. _____
   _____

3. _____
   _____

4. _____
   _____

5. _____
   _____

My health/physical goals include:

1. _____
   _____

2. _____
   _____

3. _____
   _____

4. _____
   _____

5. _____
   _____
   _____

My recreational goals include:

1. _____
_____

2. _____
_____

3. _____
_____

4. _____
_____

5. _____
_____
_____

What goals are the most important to you?

Choose two goals from each category that are the most important to you. Identify each goal as **short term (**1-4 weeks), **medium term**(2-12months), or **long term** (1 year or longer.)

1. _____

2. _____

3. _____

4. _____

5. _____

6. _____

7. _____

8. _____

9. _____

10. _____

11. _____

12. _____

Prioritize your goals

List and prioritize six of your most important goals. After each goal, identify what you could be doing now to work towards that goal and what resources you need to achieve each goal.

Goal #1_____

What I can be doing now to work toward that goal:

_____

_____

_____

The resources I need to achieve this goal are:

_____

_____

_____

Goal #2_____

What I can be doing now to work toward that goal:

_____

_____

_____

The resources I need to achieve this goal are:

_____

_____

_____

Goal
#3_____

What I can be doing now to work toward that goal:

_____

_____

_____

The resources I need to achieve this goal are:

_____

_____

_____

Goal
#4_____

What I can be doing now to work toward that goal:

_____

_____

_____

The resources I need to achieve this goal are:

_____

_____

_____

Goal
#5_____

What I can be doing now to work toward that goal:

_____

_____

_____

The resources I need to achieve this goal are:

_____

_____

_____

Goal
#6_____

What I can be doing now to work toward that goal:

_____

_____

_____

The resources I need to achieve this goal are:

_____

_____

_____

Now that you have them broken down, begin working on these goals. If you take a few steps each day, it is better than not doing it at all. Maybe you wanted to finish that writing project. Work for ½ hour every day instead of watching a show. You might want to work on your relationship with your Dad, resolve to spend an hour each weekend working with him. Whatever the goal ----work towards it!

This week we are working on goal setting. It is about making a goal and reaching it. Don't become a teenager that has no aspirations to do things. If your goal is not to attend college, which is perfectly fine, just use your skills and start gaining new ones to add to your ability. It starts now while you are young. Look to improve things around you, that is good motivation.

Week 16
Establishing a routine

Establishing a morning routine

When you establish a routine for yourself each morning, you are creating an environment of consistency. When you are part of a family, your morning routine affects your family members. With consistency comes known expectations of roles and responsibilities, known outcomes and a happier, calmer family life. How does your morning routine measure up? Ask yourself the following questions:

- Do you ever feel rushed in the mornings?
- Do you feel stressed out, when mother is cross because you slept in late?
- Do you find like you are getting distracted when trying to complete your most important tasks?
- Do you regularly feel like you have just wasted your day?

If you answered "yes' to these questions then it is time to establish a morning routine. You want your day to get off to a great start, because this will determine the sort of day you have☺

Having a morning routine means implementing and establishing a consistent routine to help create order in your home life and to help you gain control of your day.

When you have a morning routine, it usually does not involve hitting the snooze button on your alarm four times before you actually roll out of bed or scanning your phone to see what the world is up to. It involves carefully set up tasks and habits that are to be completed before you begin your day.

Why should you do all of this? Let's view your future life as the life of a successful CEO. Think about your favorite things to do in life. Do you have a certain nonprofit group, you like to involve yourself in? Is there a certain place where you like to eat at? Do you have a business that you like to frequent because of their top customer service? In our lives we are drawn to certain businesses, products, bosses, and friends because they provide consistently good food, products, leadership and friendship. If we expect value and consistency in those things, why shouldn't we expect them in our own lives? Having a morning routine is just one of those things to help give you order and calmness to your day.

Morning routine

When waking up in the morning and leaving your room, it should be in order. But what happens when you wake up late and there isn't much time for having your room be tidy? A well worked out schedule for the things you have to do before leaving the house in the morning will help to eliminate this problem.

Here are some questions that will help you figure out your morning routine:

- Do you make needless trips back and forth across the room and up and down the stairs?
- How many minutes does it take you to put your room in order and make the bed? Can you think of any way to cut down this time?

- Did you hang up your clothing the night before and leave things in order so that there are no unnecessary things to do in the morning?
- Have you planned exactly which things to do before breakfast and what to do after breakfast so that you won't waste time?
- Do you have regular morning chores that you are responsible for doing? Start them on your own, don't make your mother remind you. You are growing up to be a man, you don't need your mom reminding you of simple routine tasks.
- Do you set aside a set time to do your email and other internet outlets? This can be a huge time waster. Set aside some time during the day and stick with it to answer emails, etc.

On the following chart, make a list of what you do in the morning before and after breakfast. Show this to your Mom and let her offer help in areas that can be improved upon. After getting advice, try and experiment every morning until you have worked out the most satisfactory schedule. A schedule that becomes a habit for everyday.   Fill in the following information and evaluate where you stand for orderliness.

Time I wake up:_____

I hit the snooze how many times:_____ eliminate this step, don't set your alarm so early if you are going to push the snooze button. Train yourself to get up as soon as it goes off.

First thing I do, after I open my eyes:_____

Should I eliminate this step: yes or no

My next steps are:
1. _____
2. _____
3. _____
4. _____
5. _____

What do I do after I have breakfast:_____

What are some things I need to do differently:
1. _____
2. _____
3. _____
4. _____
5. _____

Now that you have written out what you do, can you put into effect what you are going to change? List your "new" wake up schedule here:

My new wake up schedule is:

Time I wake up:_____

First thing I am going to do after I wake
up:_____

My next new steps are:
   1.   _____
   2.   _____
   3.   _____
   4.   _____
   5.   _____

After breakfast I will:_____

Put these into effect all week, establish a new morning routine. If your body and mind knows what to expect, things will roll much smoother in your day.

Regular household chores

Do you have a regular schedule of cleaning or tasks that you are expected to carry out each week? Your assignment is to make a schedule showing what you do each day in the week. Record the number of minutes or hours that you spend each week helping with the housework.

Take into consideration the following:

- Do you only do the things that you are asked to do in helping at home?
- Do you think to offer to do extra things so that your mother or father may have a little relief or fun?
- Do you do your share of the work willingly and pleasantly?
- Do you have to be reminded constantly of your responsibilities?

You can save time cleaning and caring for your home. This will allow more time in your day.   The most important thing is to have a plan for doing your work so that you eliminate needless steps and motions.

Sometimes when cleaning several rooms it is better to do all the sweeping, then do all the dusting, etc. Sometimes it is better to dust, sweep, and finish each room as you go. Try different ways of doing your cleaning and find the quickest way of doing your work.

You will find that if you have followed the daily practice of keeping your room in order, it is much less of a task to clean it each week. There won't be any shoes on the floor, no clothes to pick up, and no trash on your desk. Some people will have a general rule of order when it comes to cleaning a bedroom. Here is a sample to follow that will help you to do it quickly and thoroughly.

1. Wash the sheets and air the bed each week. Do this early enough to allow the bed time to air out.
2. Bring all the tools you need to clean your room. This is another way to help save wasteful time.
3. Dust and wipe down all tabletop areas in your room at least once per week. Wipe down all media screens, keyboards, etc.
4. Empty the waste basket at least once per week.
5. Cleaning the floor is last. Sweep, vacuum, or wash as needed.

This week, I want you to create a schedule for normal weekly chores that you are responsible for. Write down what chores you are to do each day. Then if you are to do certain chores once per week, I want you to schedule those as well. You may have chores that you are responsible for once a month, schedule those too.

Here is a sample schedule:

My daily chores:

Make bed

Pick up room

Wash breakfast dishes

take out the trash

My weekly chores:

Monday—wash bedding

Tuesday—clean up the yard/ leaf blow driveway

Wednesday—clean out the garage

Thursday—clean van

Friday—deep clean bathroom

Saturday—clean out animal pens

Make a list of your daily chores, then your weekly chores. If you have many chores that you do only once per week, divide them up among each day. That way you are not cramming all of your work into one day.

You can do this type of scheduling with every area of your life. If you are doing your school work, schedule exactly when you are to complete it. Schedule in time for extra activities like writing, exercising, woodworking, fishing or building projects.. Maybe choose a different day each week to focus on different tasks(ex: woodworking on Monday, fishing on Tues, etc.) Make sure to throw in some free time as well. Stick to your schedule. If you have a different schedule each day, write it all out. This way you will know what is expected out of your day and when thinking about what it is you need to be doing, you can look at your schedule. Don't cram up your entire day, leave some flexibility for when life gets crazy. The key is to establish some sort of order.

Your goal is to eliminate wasted time. You want to be efficient at what you do. Remember when you take less time to do daily and weekly habits, that leaves more time for fun and freedom.

My daily chores:

_____

_____

_____

_____

_____

_____

My weekly chores:

Mon_____

Tues_____

Wed_____

Thurs_____

Fri_____

Sat_____

Week 17
Avoiding clutter

Have nothing in your houses that you do not know to be useful or believe to be beautiful." – William Morris

For some of you, you may have grown up in a cluttered home. A place where cupboards would not close, closets and dressers were overflowing with clothing, and stuff was shoved under the beds and into nooks and crannies. When guests came over it was a huge chore to clean the house and everyone had to help because it was such a big job. Does that sound all too familiar?

Most people don't even notice that they have too much stuff. It is something that is overlooked. But day after day they are spending hours trying to get ahead of housecleaning and organizing. They are constantly making an excuse as to why their home is in disarray. The answer is very simple of what they need to do to help those issues....they need to declutter!

To understand the definition of declutter, we need to define what "clutter" is:

> *to fill up or possibly cover with dispersed or disordered items that obstruct movement as well as minimize effectiveness.*

Therefore, declutter is the opposite action. It really is to sort items and get tidy. It means to order items, to put things in place where they belong.

Most peoples' homes are full of things. We live in a land of "stuff." Stuff that makes us feel good, stuff that we don't want to get rid of, and stuff that takes over our lives.

It begins when we own too many things. When we have fewer items the easier it will be to keep clutter at a minimum.

The first and easiest ways to start decluttering is to remove the excessive possessions that are stealing our lives, times, and energy.

In your process of removing the excess, it can be helpful to define what it is that is causing your clutter. Usually it is defined in 3 ways:

1. Too much stuff in too small of a space
2. Anything that you no longer use or like
3. Anything that leads to a feeling of disorganization

It is not good to have too many things in your room. A few well arranged items on top of your dresser make it much easier to keep order and will help you save time in caring for your room.

Questions to consider:

- How is your desk looking?
- Is it cluttered and untidy looking?
- Are there books that you don't regularly use that are left out?
- Are there things on the top of the table that should be kept in drawers or boxes?
- What other places in your room may be in disorder and full of unnecessary things?

Putting things away

Having a convenient place for everything is important for time management. But it is only part of the solution, the other part is to actually put things in their places.

It is much easier and saves time if you do not drop things just anywhere you feel like dropping them in your room.   If you put things away and hang up your clothes at night, there will be no picking up to do in the morning.

The habit of putting things away instead of putting things down is your new goal.

You need to emphasize doing the tasks that will take you less than two minutes to put away, right away. Otherwise that small job will turn into an *"add it to my to do list later"* item. The more that we can get done in the moment, the less we will have to remember to do them again later.

This principle can be adapted to be even more powerful when you get into the habit of using it beyond physical items in your room or home, but also with digital information and follow-up tasks.

Let's say you receive an invite for an upcoming party, if you are able to attend, RSVP now, not later. Then mark it on your calendar and throw away the invite. What about emails that comes into your box and needs information attended to? Reply right away, and then you can clear your inbox. Letting your inbox fill up with email is just like leaving items on the countertop because you don't want to put them away now.

One of my favorite sayings is,

"Never put off till tomorrow, what you can do today."

Use that even in the littlest of applications in life. If you can put away all your items after returning from a shopping trip now, then do it. Don't wait till a later time to put things away. Why wait? Stop procrastinating and just get it done.

Hands on skill this week:

You are going to take note to pay attention to immediately getting done what can be done, instead of waiting until a later time. Apply this principle when returning home from being gone all day, when you complete activities and have to put large amounts of stuff away, and as you go about your daily life. Look at each opportunity to get things done, instead of waiting for a later date.

Are you noticing that you are more apt to just dropping your items and leaving them for a later time? Are you stopping and reminding yourself that instead of putting things down, I need to put them away?

Work this week at being consistent at putting things away immediately instead of waiting for a later time. Do not put off for later which you can do right now. Take the extra two minutes and get it done.

Which tasks, that can be completed in just a few moments, do you put off "till a later time?" Write these tasks down. If you cannot think of any, just ask others in your family which ones they think you need to improve. Sometimes others can see things that we might not see.

Tasks I need to improve upon doing immediately:
  1. _____
  2. _____
  3. _____
  4. _____
  5. _____

Hands on skill:

You are going to declutter your room. Decluttering is a constant thing otherwise things will accumulate quickly. You may have already done this in the beginning, that is okay, you can do this many times throughout the year, it keeps things neat.

Here are some simple steps to declutter your room:

1. Clear a working area probably in the middle, where you can sort things. Gather a bag for trash, boxes for donate and return to other areas of the home.
2. Work in a clock pattern around your room start at 12 and move around the room in a clockwise pattern.
3. Do one drawer or shelf at a time.
4. Pull everything out of the drawer or shelf and set it in your working area. Sort the items into the appropriate places— trash, give away, or return to the drawer or shelf.
5. When deciding where each item should go you need to make an instant decision. Think about when was the last time you used this? If you haven't used it for six months or more you probably won't. Exceptions to seasonal items.
6. Continue to work on your entire room until you return back to the 12 o'clock mark.

If this is the first time that you have decluttered your room, it will probably take a few hours. Work in sections if it seems to overwhelm you. Take a break and do something else in between. The more that you do this, it will normally only take an hour or so to upkeep your room.

When setting up your dresser, think what items you absolutely need to leave out and put the rest away.

The same is true for your desks and nightstands. You can only read one book at a time. Place the other ones away and out of sight.

Week 18
Wrap up

There are many resources out there for you as a young man to develop into manhood.

You want good counsel and godly direction. If you can't get that sort of guidance from your home life, seek to find another gentleman that would be willing to mentor and teach you some skills.

I am recommending a few books that I have all my boys read. I don't require them to read much, but these I do:

- Daily reading of the Bible—nothing is going to benefit you more in life than God's word. Establish a daily reading and make it part of your normal everyday routine.
- Created for Work by Bob Schultz
- Practical Happiness by Bob Schultz
- Boyhood and Beyond by Bob Schultz
- I kissed dating goodbye by Joshua Harris

These last few books are short chapters, ones that you can read within 15-20 minutes each day. They are packed full of godly men wisdom and if followed will help you develop into a godly man.

Check through your local library and if not, invest the small amount to purchase these, they are well worth your time.

Look to watch movies that keep sexual purity and a Godly standard.

I like to watch some reality shows that still keep the "old fashioned" approach to courtship. This lets my children know that there are other children out there that are striving for the same ideals. It is nice that the media doesn't portray the old fashioned as uncool and plain. They actually show them as successful, happy, individuals.

I am also very happy to find that there are youtubers that stand for remaining pure until marriage and they are successful on YouTube. I mentioned this because YouTube is a big part of the younger generation.

Everything in life is a choice. You make the choice to decide what to watch, what to read, what to look at on your phone, even if you think things are done in secret, there are no secrets. Every time you try and hide that part of your life away by watching ungodly things, it tears apart pieces of your soul. Keep your heart and soul intact and ready for your future spouse by remaining pure. Make the commitment to follow after Christ and to allow him to find you your perfect mate.

What you can do right now, is to start preparing yourself for your future. What sort of future do you want to have? Do you want to be successful? Have a good wife? Have a nice home? Nice car? All that begins with the decision you make now. If you want to be successful with nice things, you are going to have to learn how to work hard at making money to get them. If you want a nice wife, you are going to have to work hard at making yourself be a "good gentleman". How nice for your future spouse to find out that you have been praying for and working towards the day when you would meet. How blessed she will be to find out that you have remained pure and saved all of your heart and emotions for only her. She will feel very special to know that you have been waiting for the day when you two would connect.

When the day comes and you can ask her father permission to court her, when he asks how you think you will support her financially, and you can confidently say how financially set you are. Because you have been diligent with your money from day one. You know what your financial plans are, you know what you are going to do for employment, and you are confident that you can supply materially for a family on your own. That will say a lot about your character to him and to your future spouse.

Being prepared is the key in life. A young man who decides to take this path is going to be far greater ahead than his counterparts who choose to live for the moment. It takes making that decision to choose this path of life. We all have a choice, which one will you choose?

Made in the USA
Columbia, SC
06 January 2022

53693285R00100